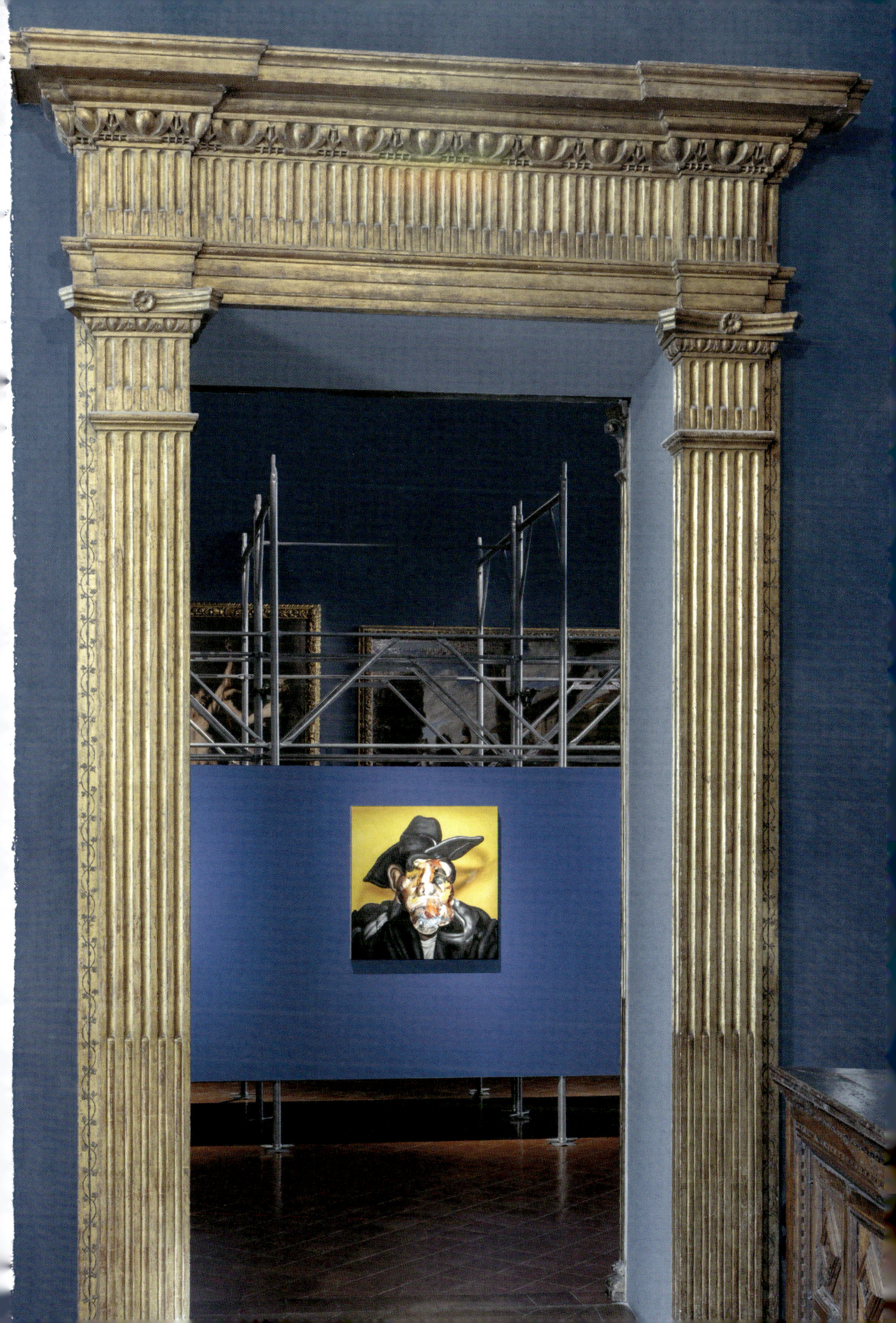

Rabbit Man
2022
oil paint, oil pastel,
gouache on linen canvas
stretched over wood panel
91.4 × 91.4 cm
Private collection, Europe

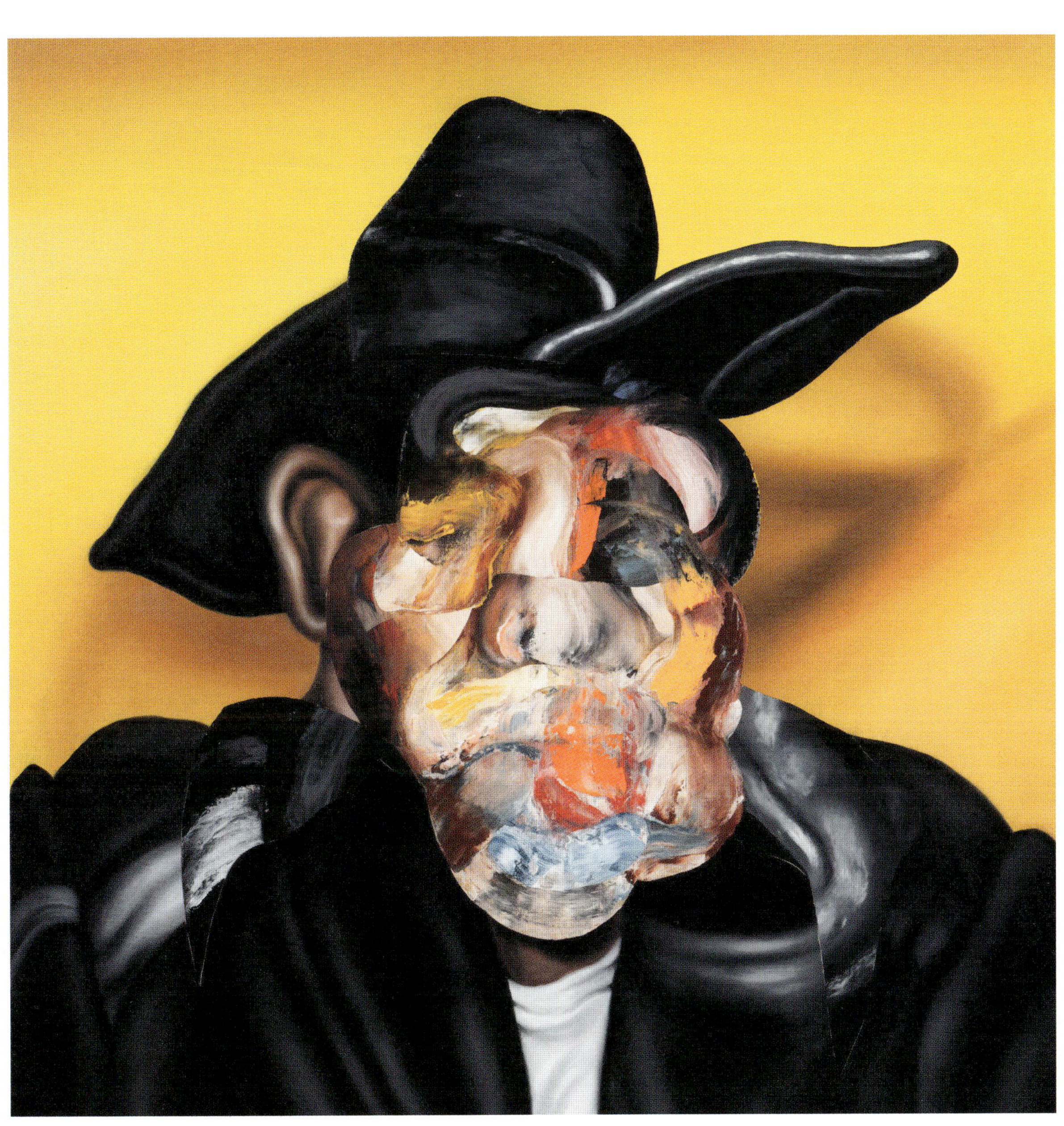

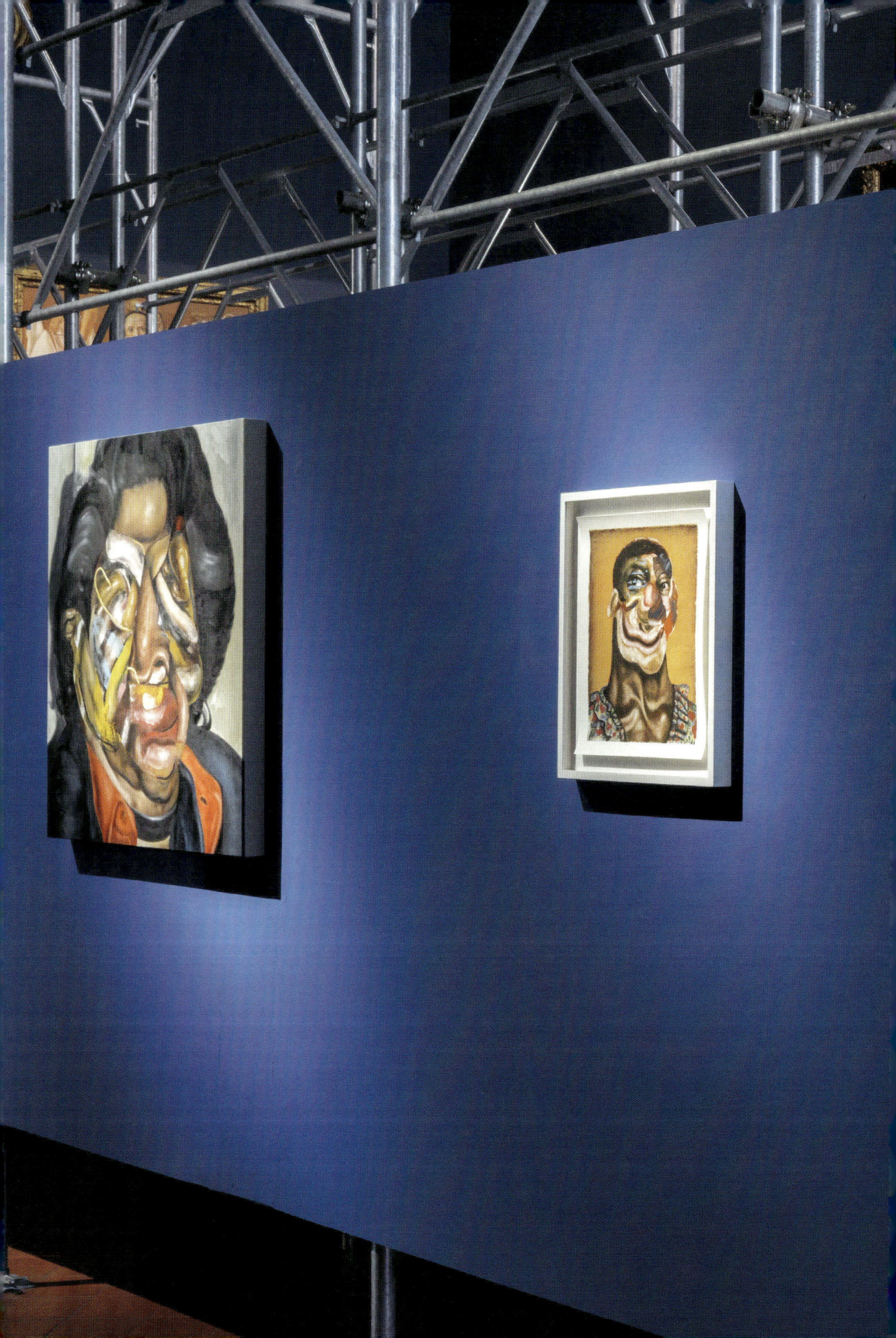

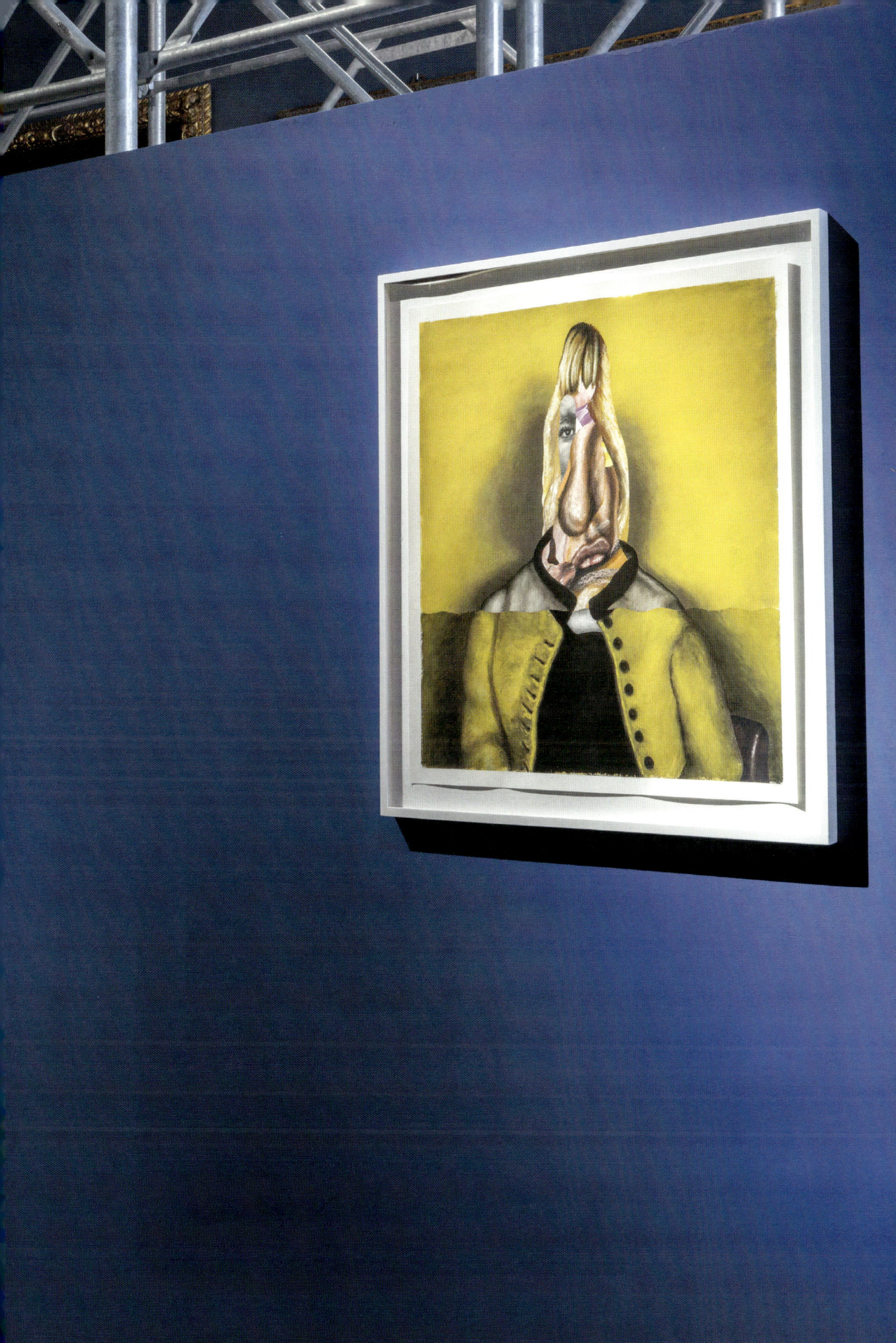

Mama, Joe, and James Brown
2023
oil paint, oil pastel, soft pastel,
gouache on linen canvas
stretched over wood panel
91.4 × 91.4 cm
Private collection, London

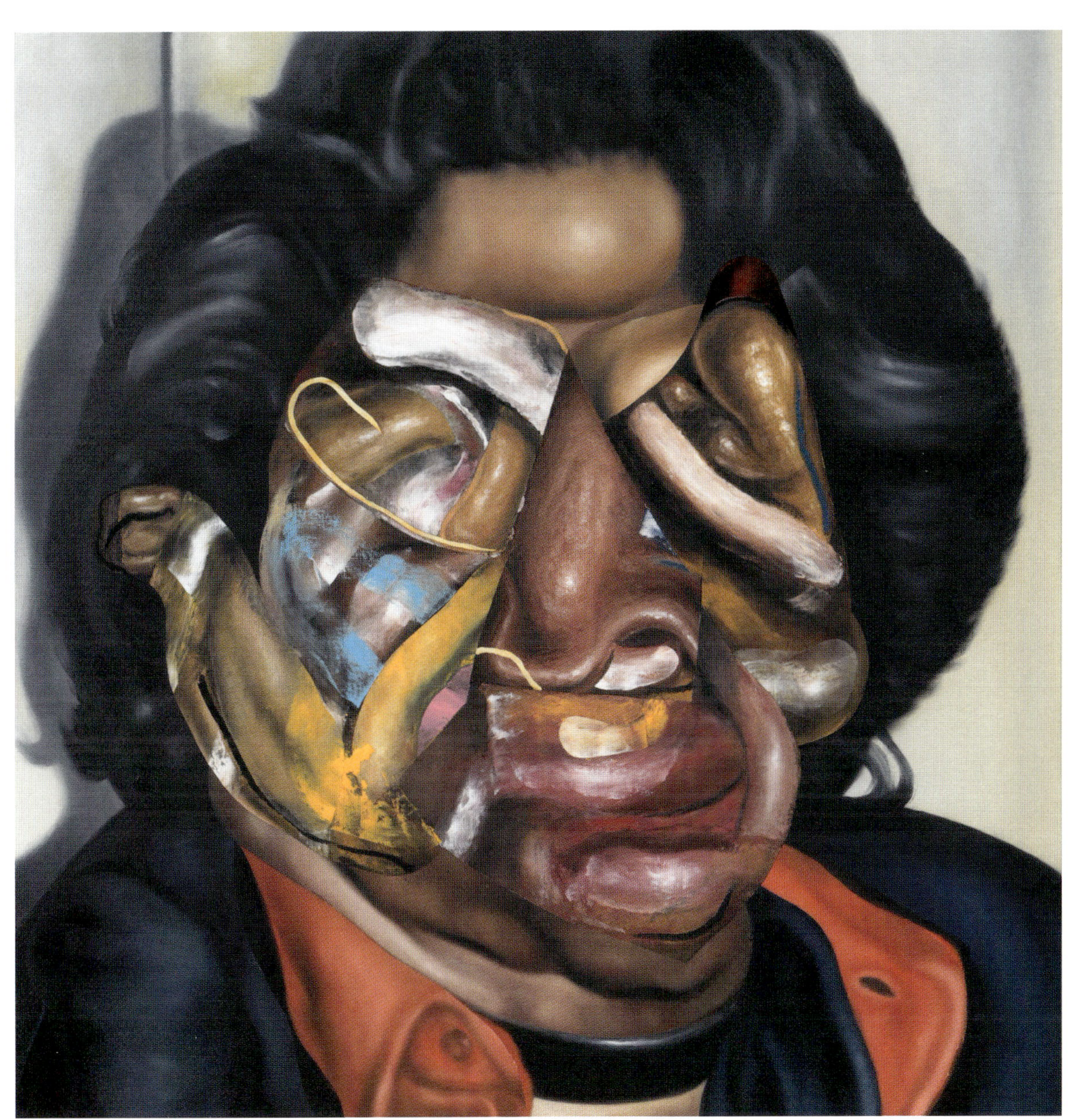

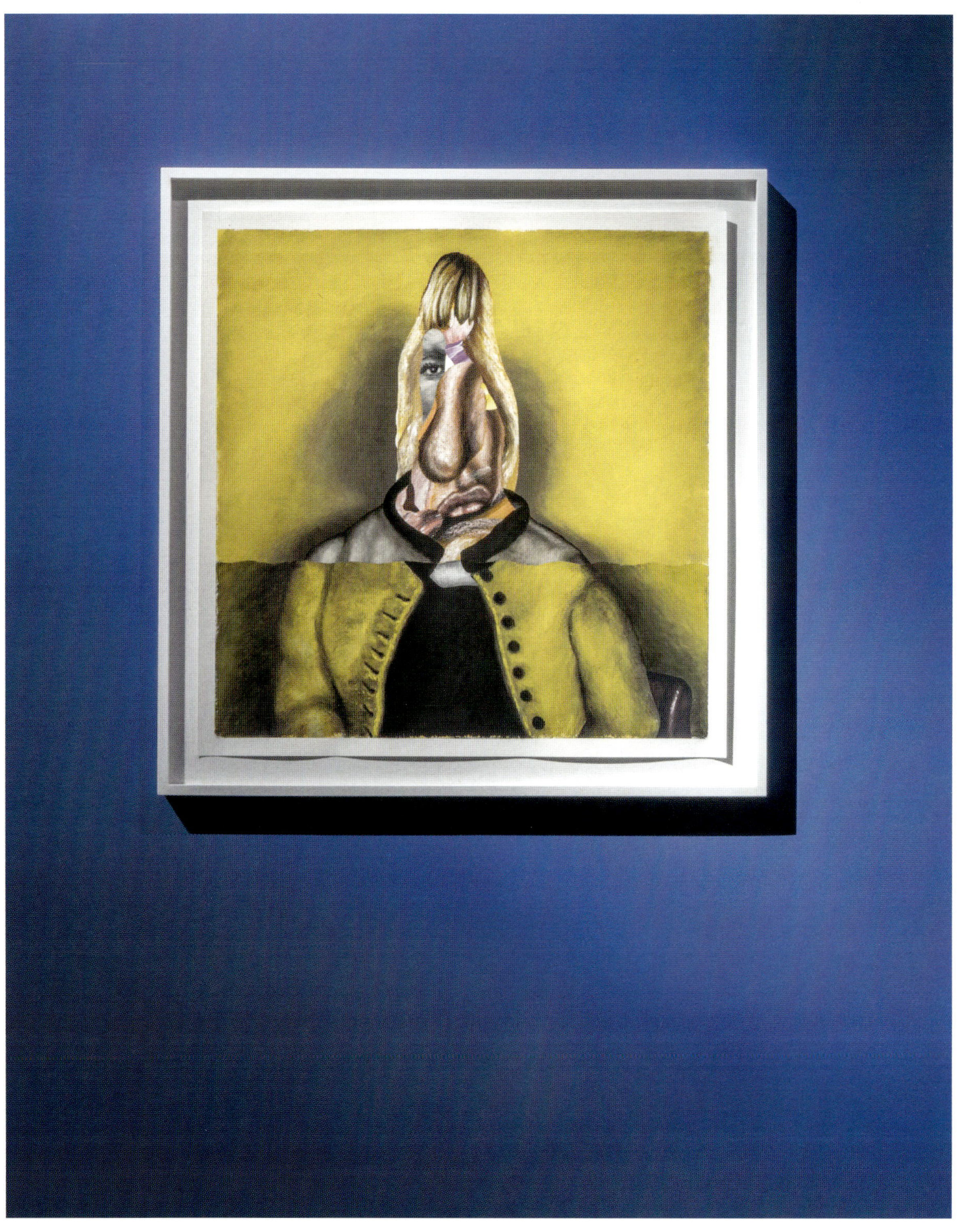

The Executive Director
2019
black charcoal, gouache,
soft pastel on Coventry
Vellum paper
76.2 × 76.2 cm
Private collection, Luxembourg

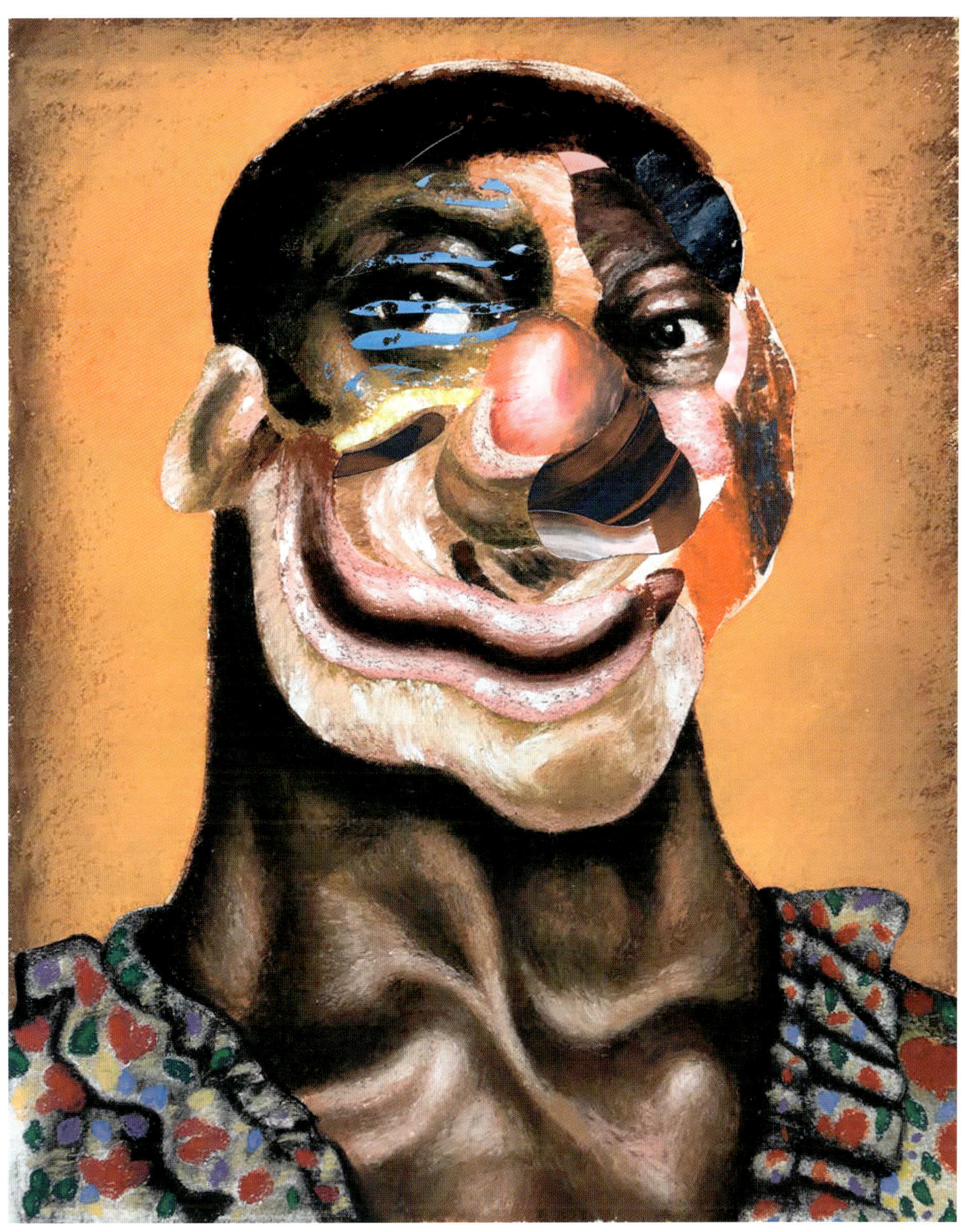

The Grinning Chef
2019
black charcoal, gouache,
soft pastel, oil pastel on Coventry
Vellum paper
42 × 35 cm
Private collection

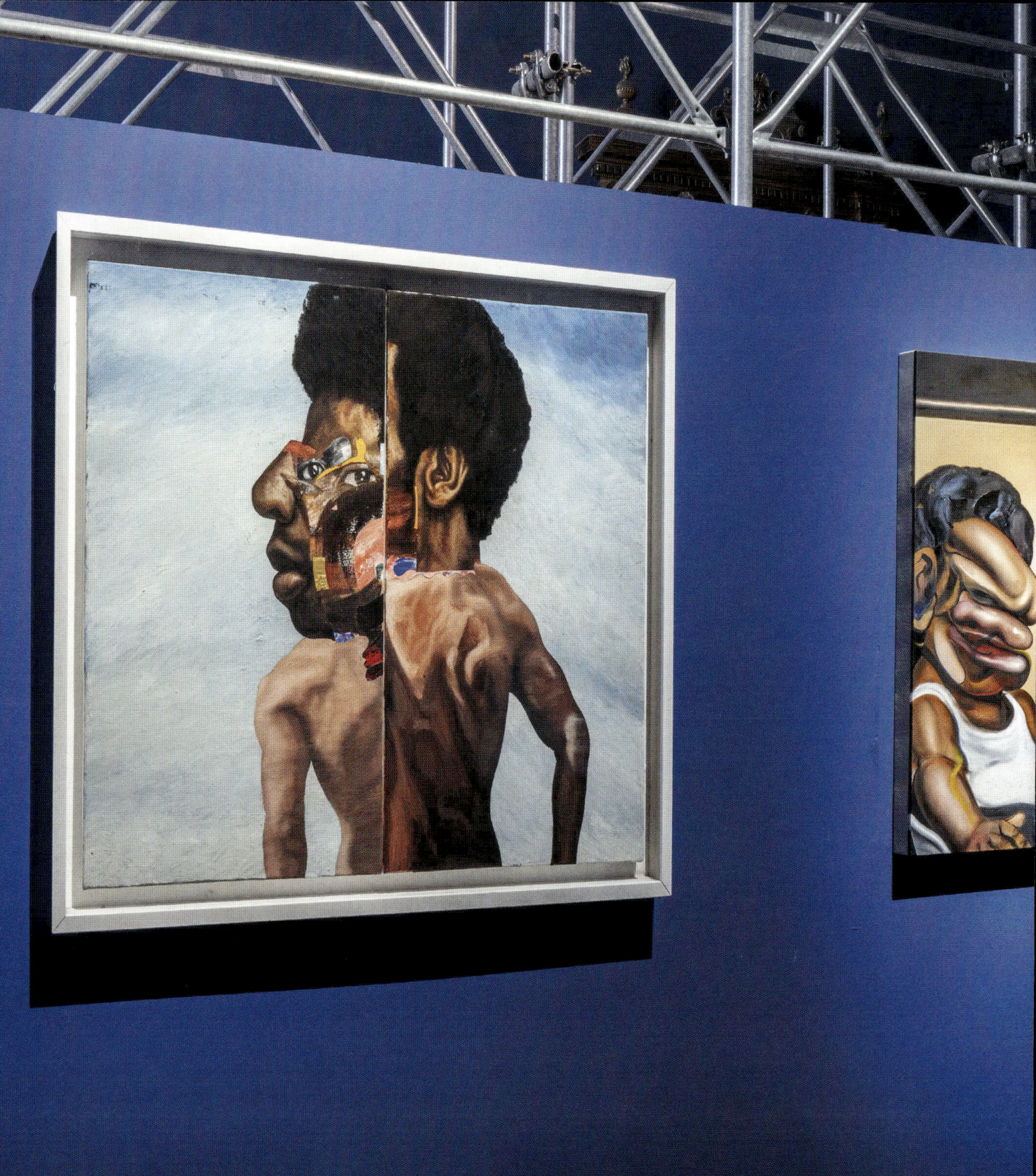

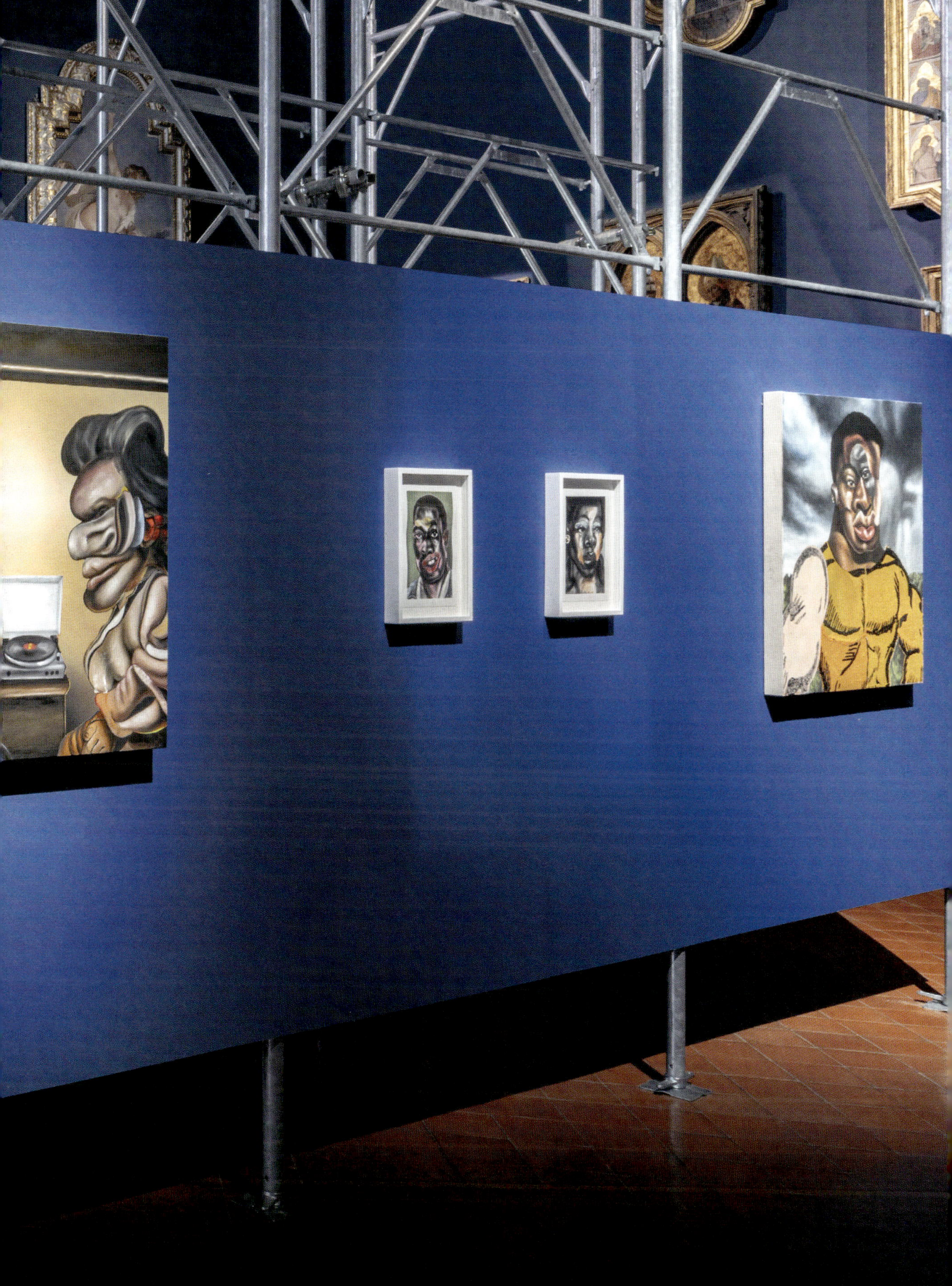

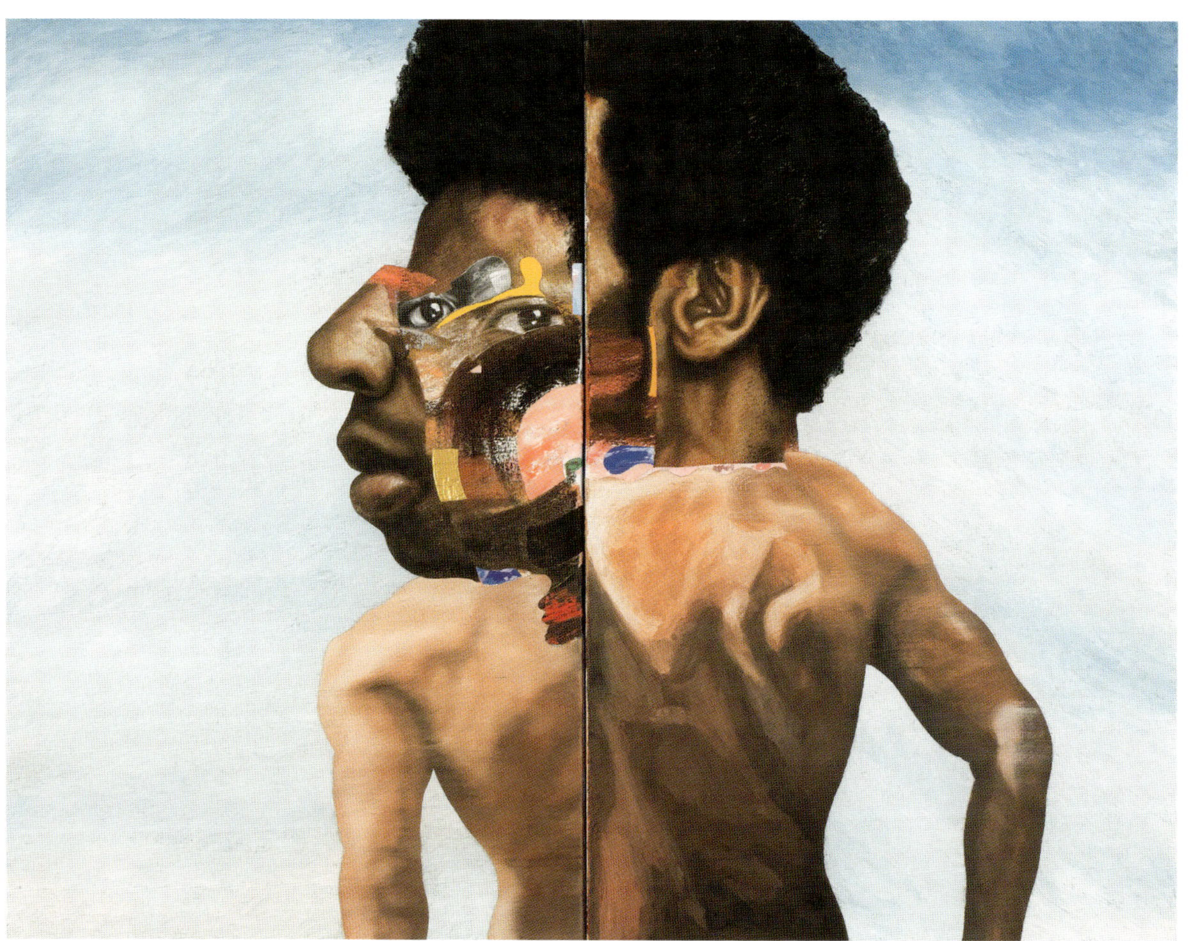

There He Went
2017
black charcoal, gouache,
soft pastel, oil pastel, oil paint,
paint stick, acrylic gold powder
on canvas
91.4 × 121.9 cm
Collection of Alexander DiPersia

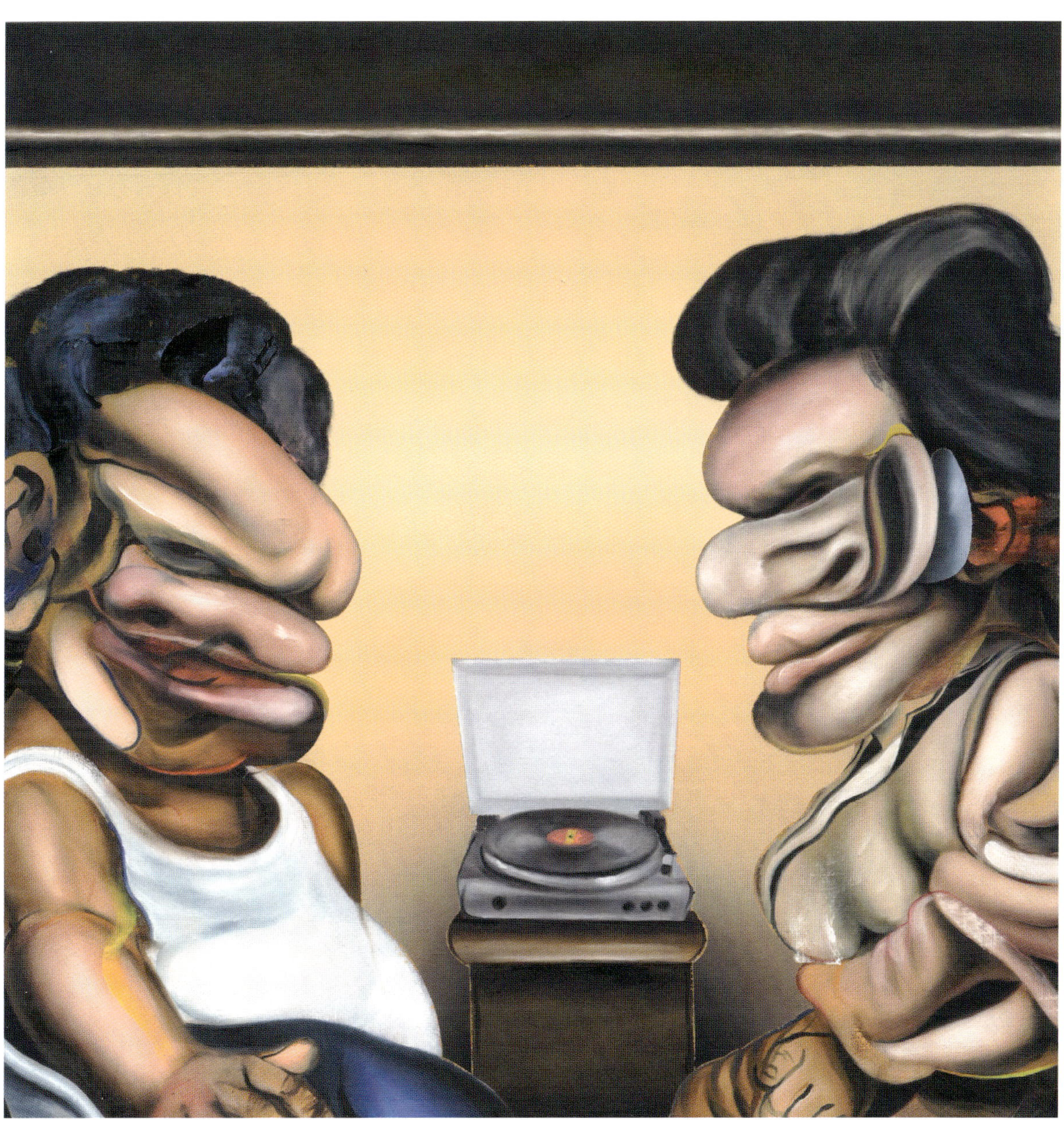

The Record Player
2023
oil paint on linen canvas stretched
over wood panel
91.4 × 91.4 cm
Courtesy the Artist and Gagosian

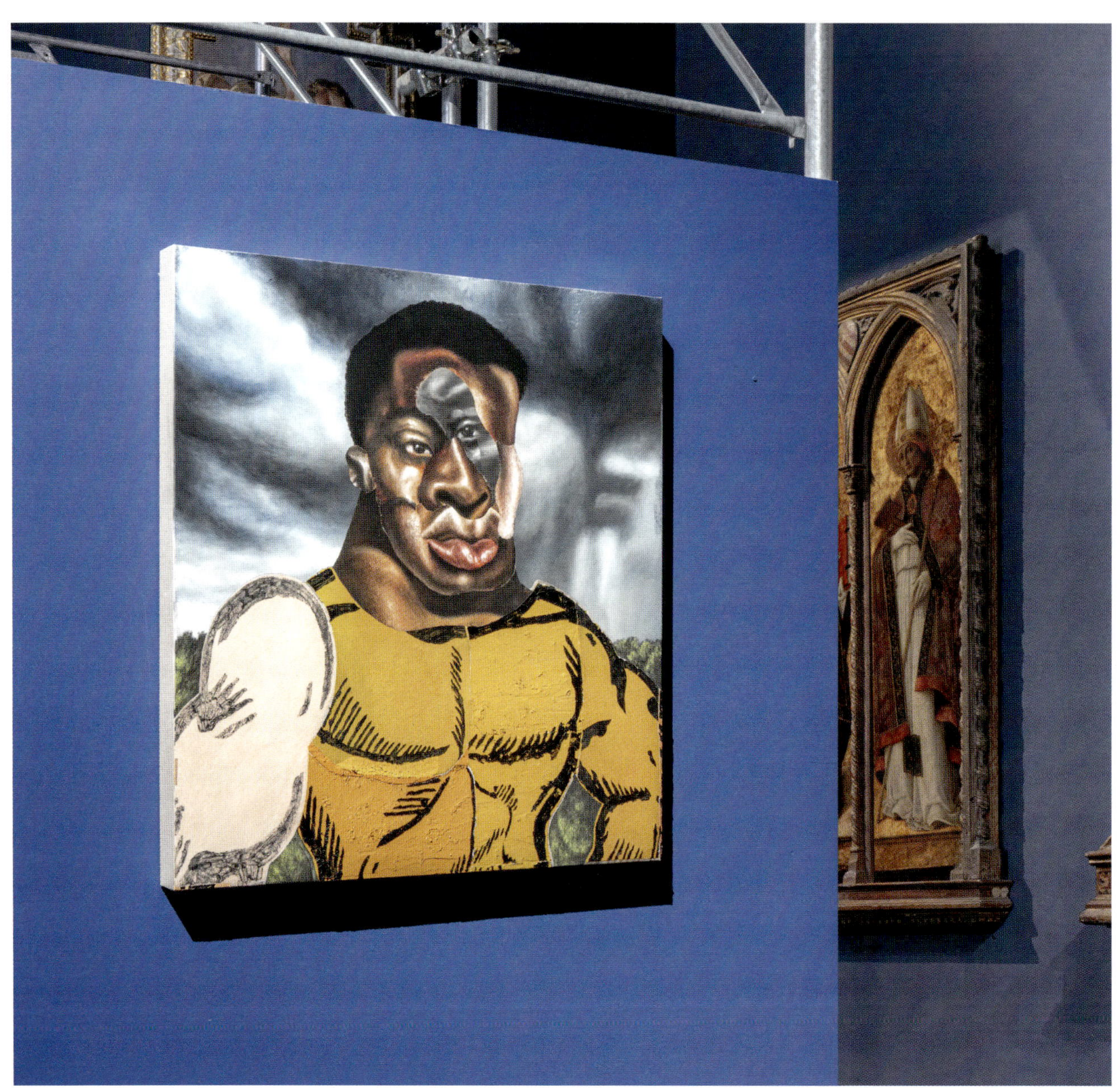

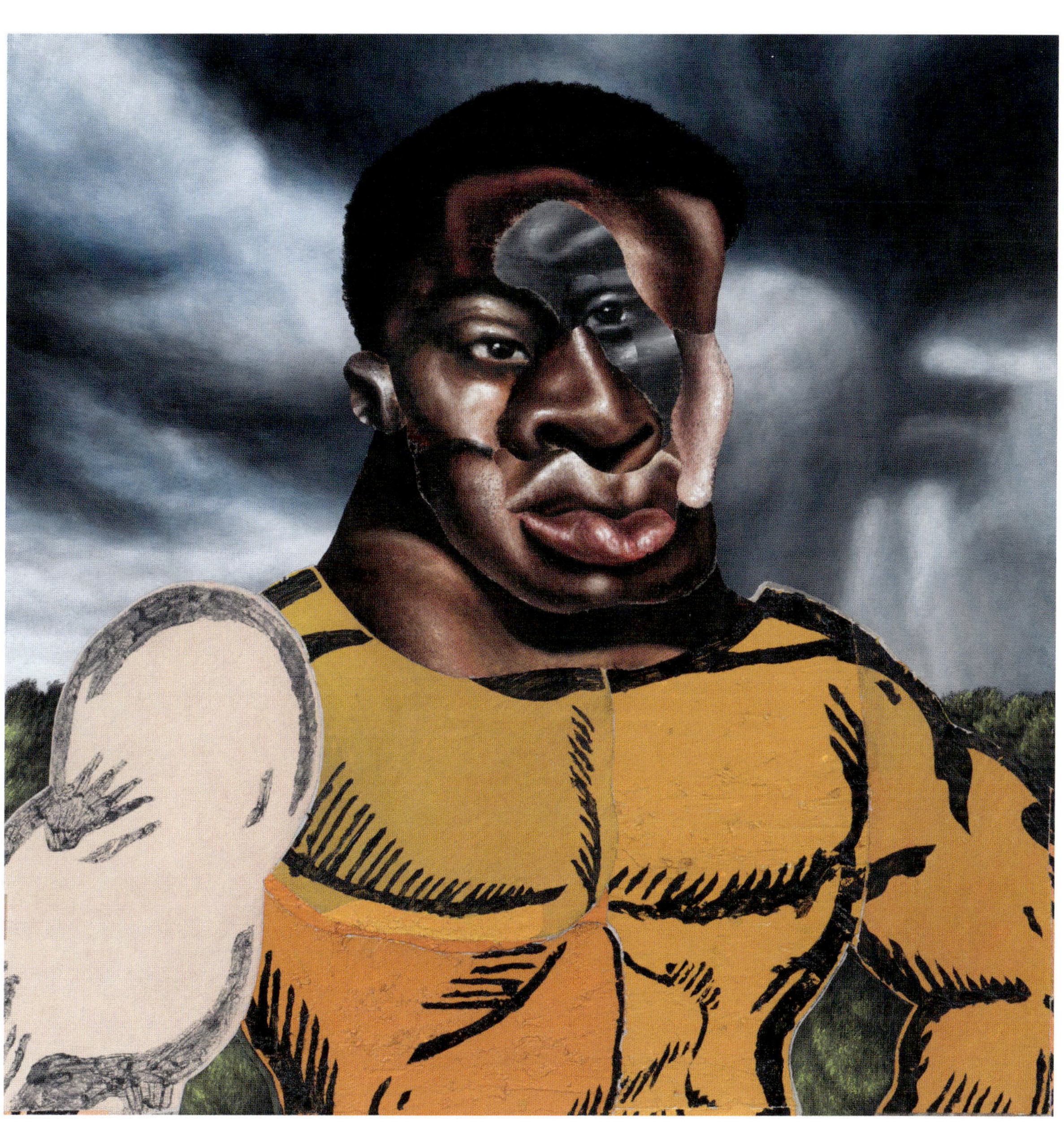

Mr. Nightmare
2020
oil paint, paint stick, oil pastel,
soft pastel, gouache,
black charcoal on linen canvas
stretched over wood panel
91.4 × 91.4 cm
Meïjer Family Collection

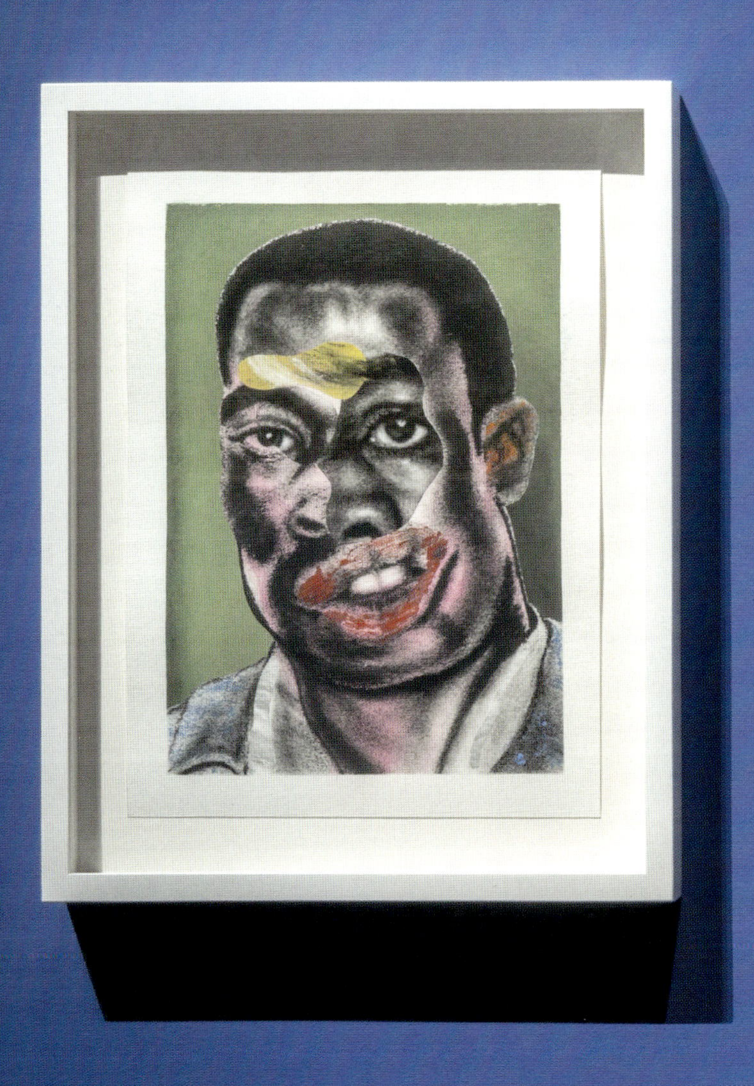

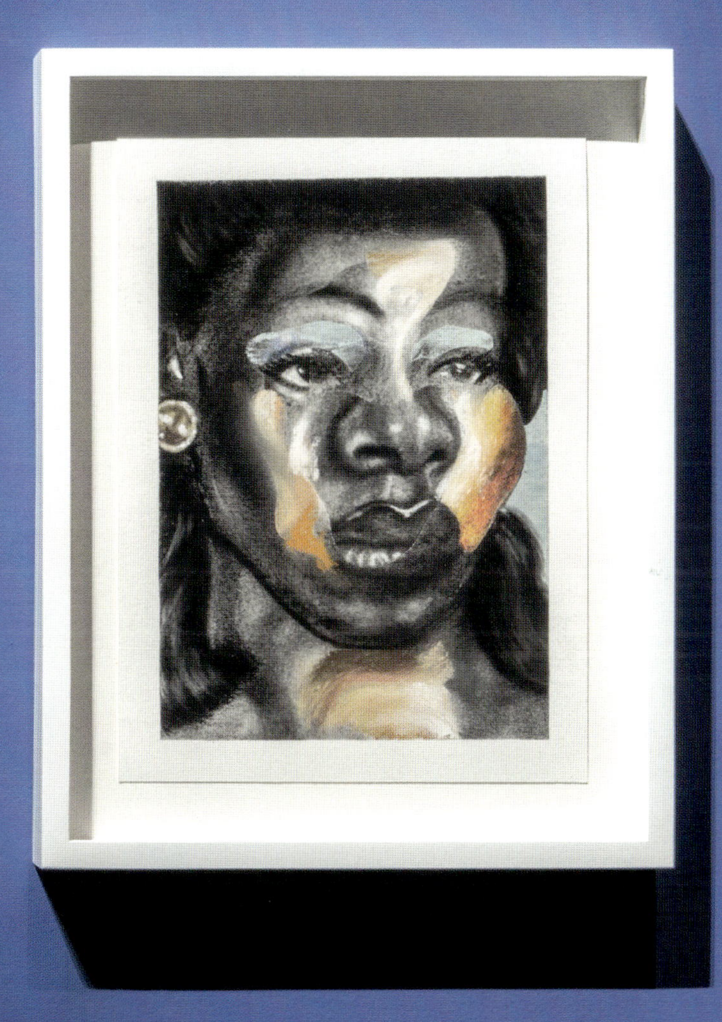

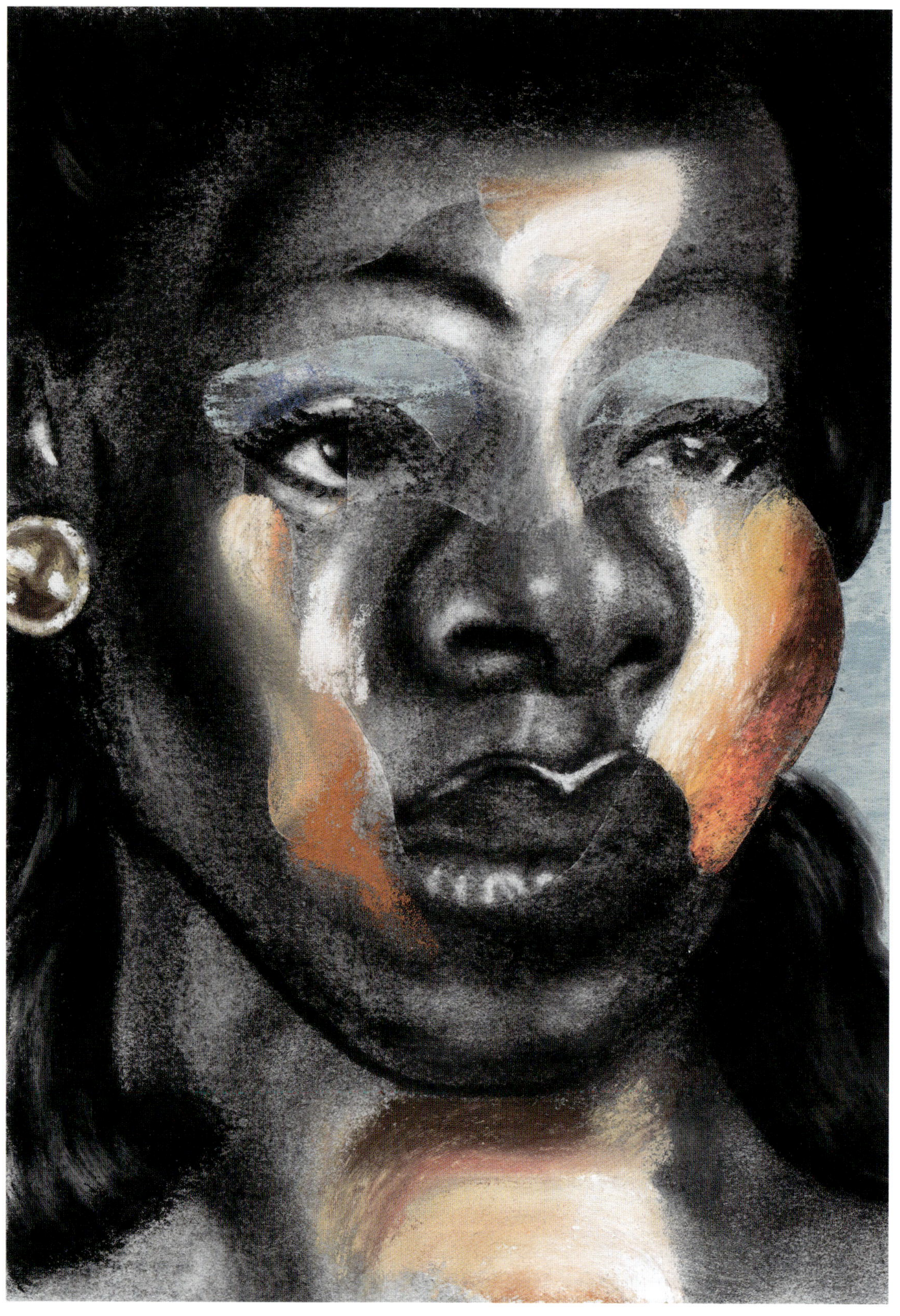

Butterfly
2020
black charcoal, gouache,
soft pastel on Coventry
Vellum paper
30.5 × 22.9 cm
Private collection, London

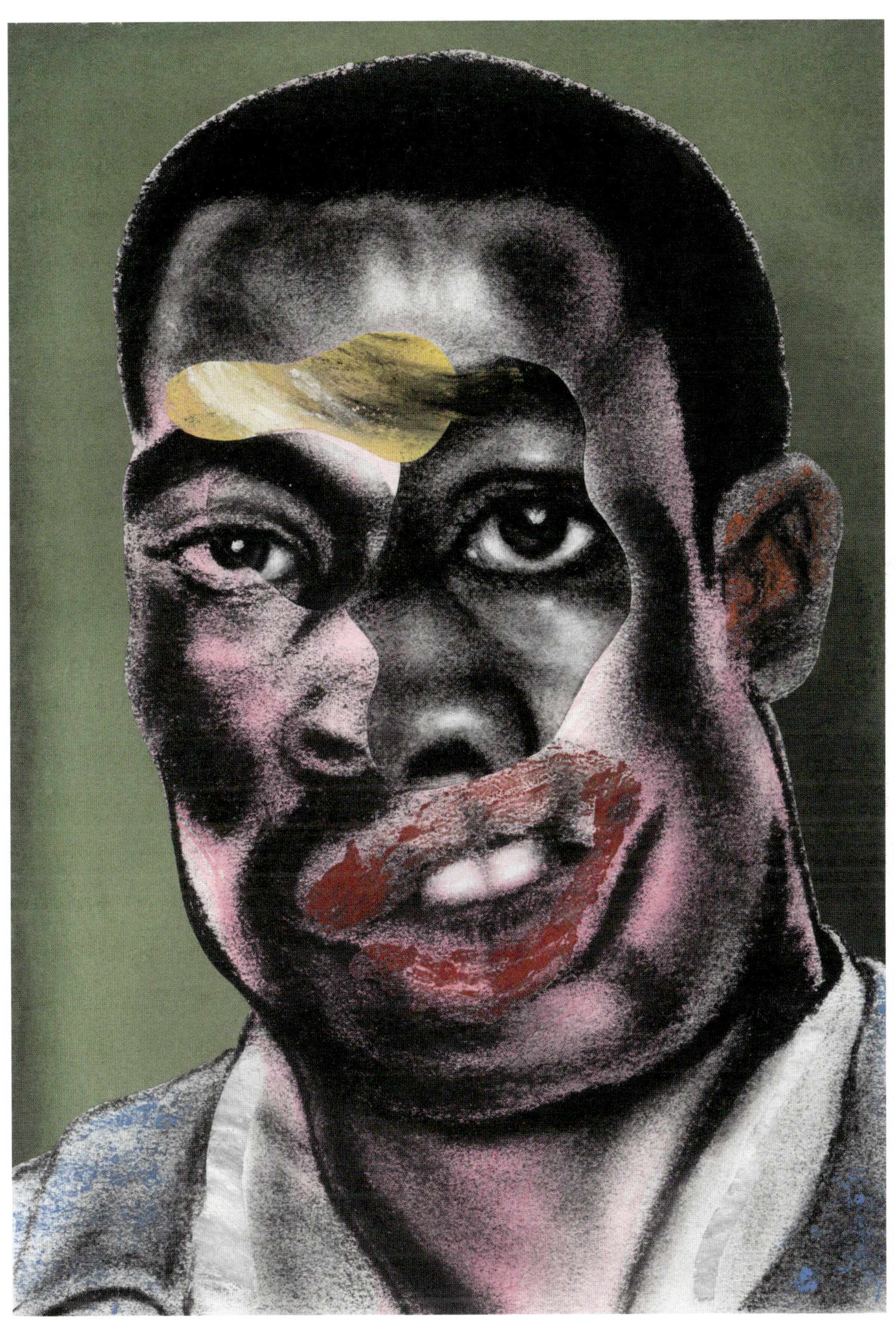

Heavy Eyes
2020
black charcoal,
gouache, soft pastel
on Coventry Vellum paper
30.5 × 22.9 cm
Château La Coste Collection

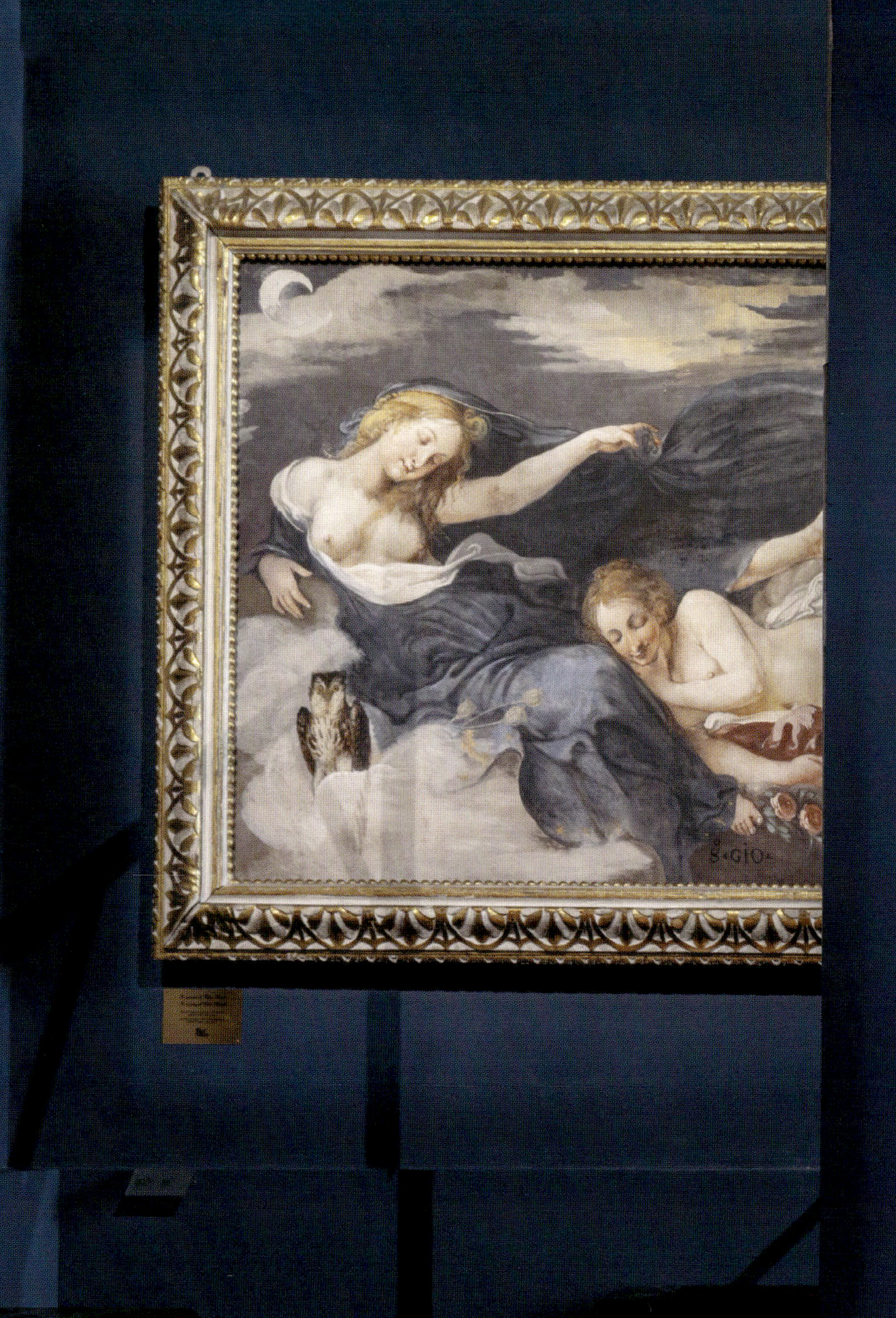

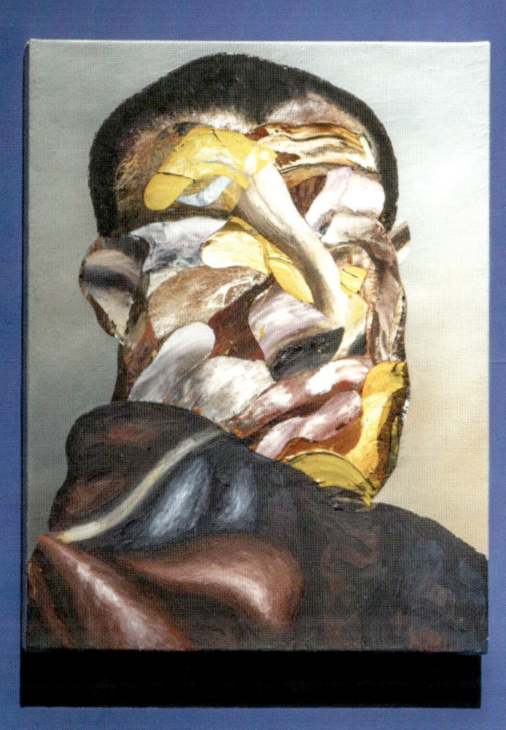

The Break
2019
oil paint, paint stick, oil pastel,
soft pastel, gouache on linen
canvas stretched over wood panel
45.7 × 35.6 cm
Collection of Alexander DiPersia

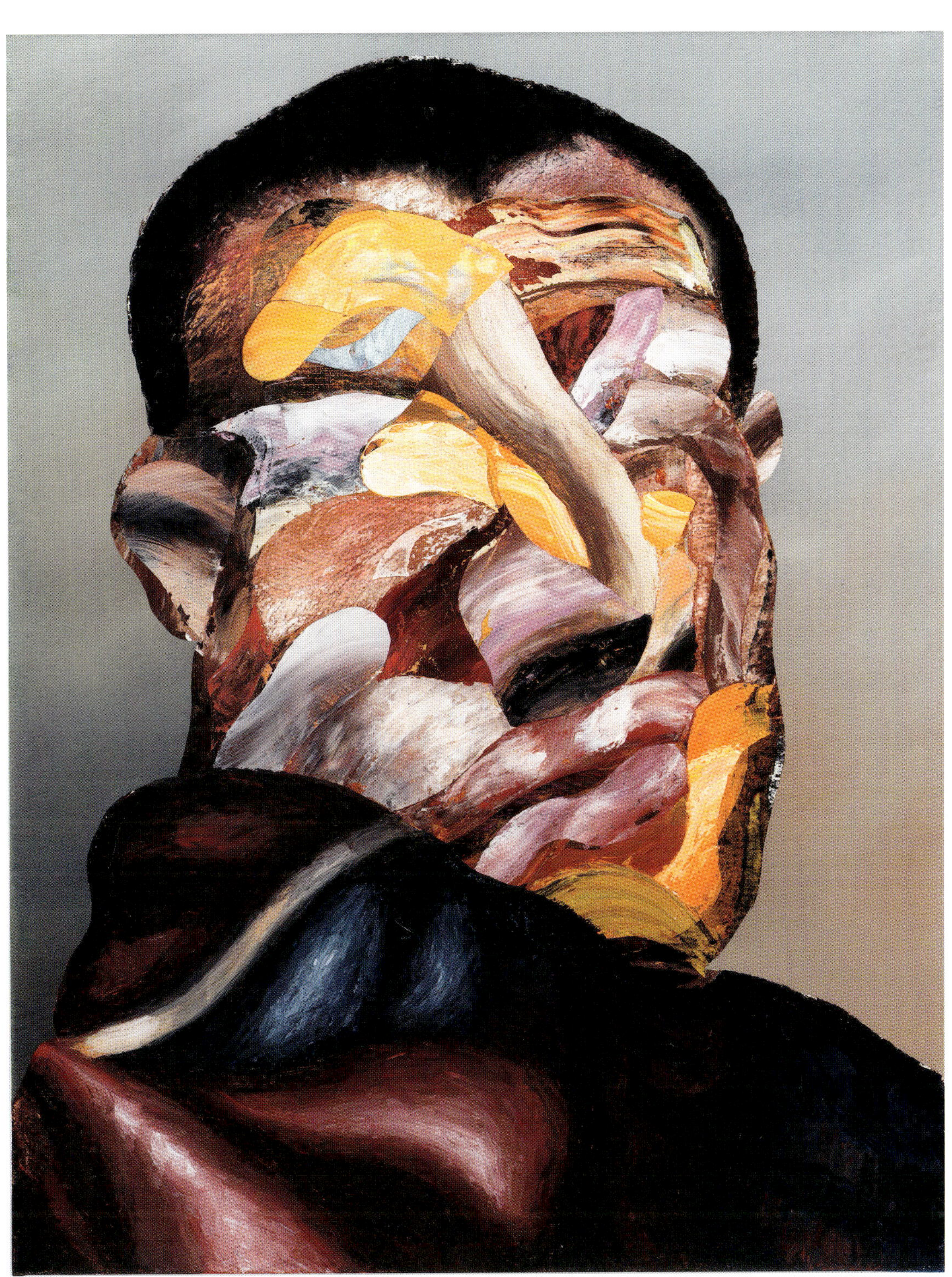

After Pontormo's Portrait
of Alessandro de' Medici
2023
oil paint, oil pastel,
gouache on linen canvas
stretched over wood panel
50.8 × 40.6 cm
Courtesy the Artist and Gagosian

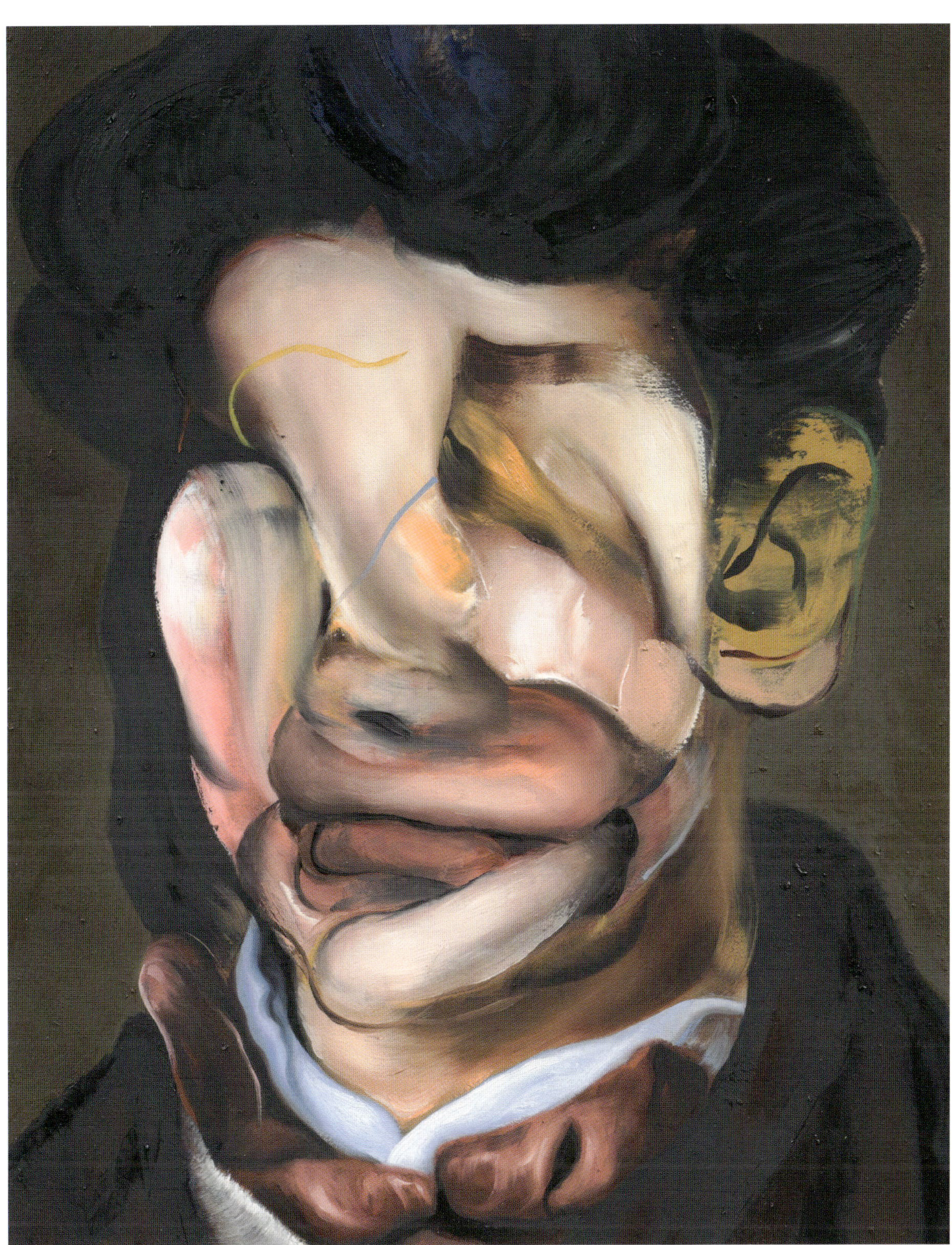

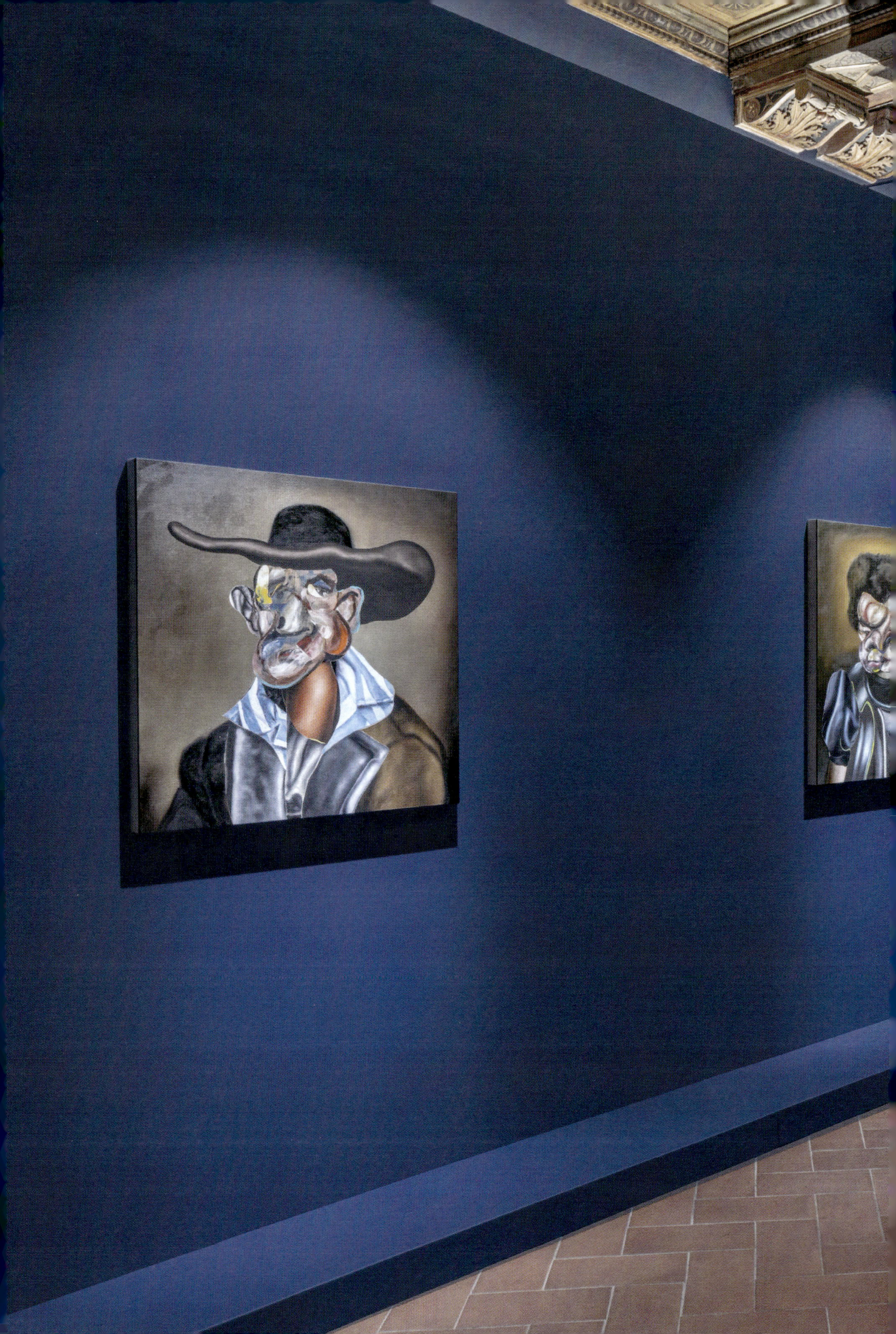

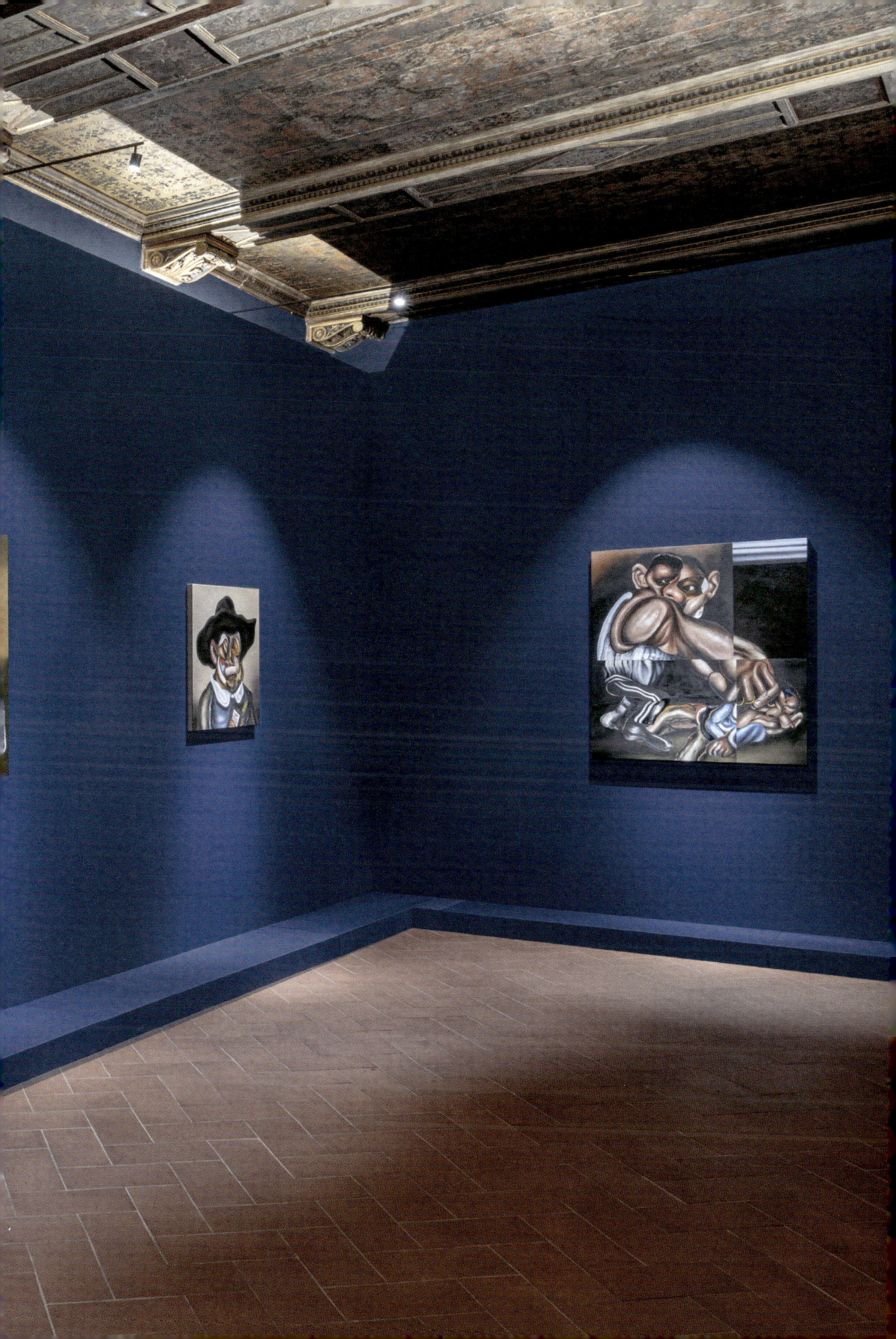

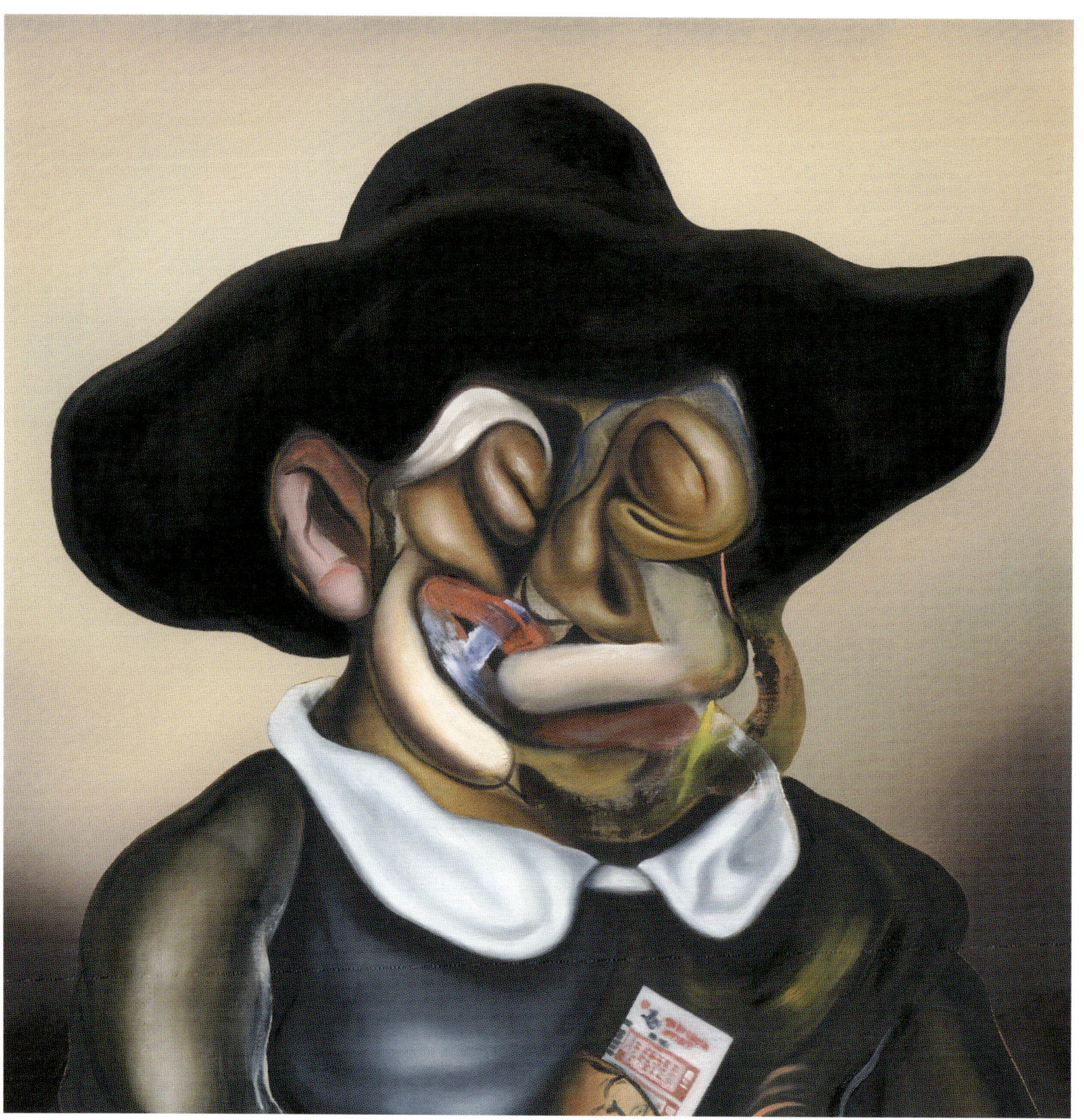

The Lottery Ticket
2023
oil paint on linen canvas
stretched over wood panel
76.2 × 76.2 cm
Courtesy the Artist and Gagosian

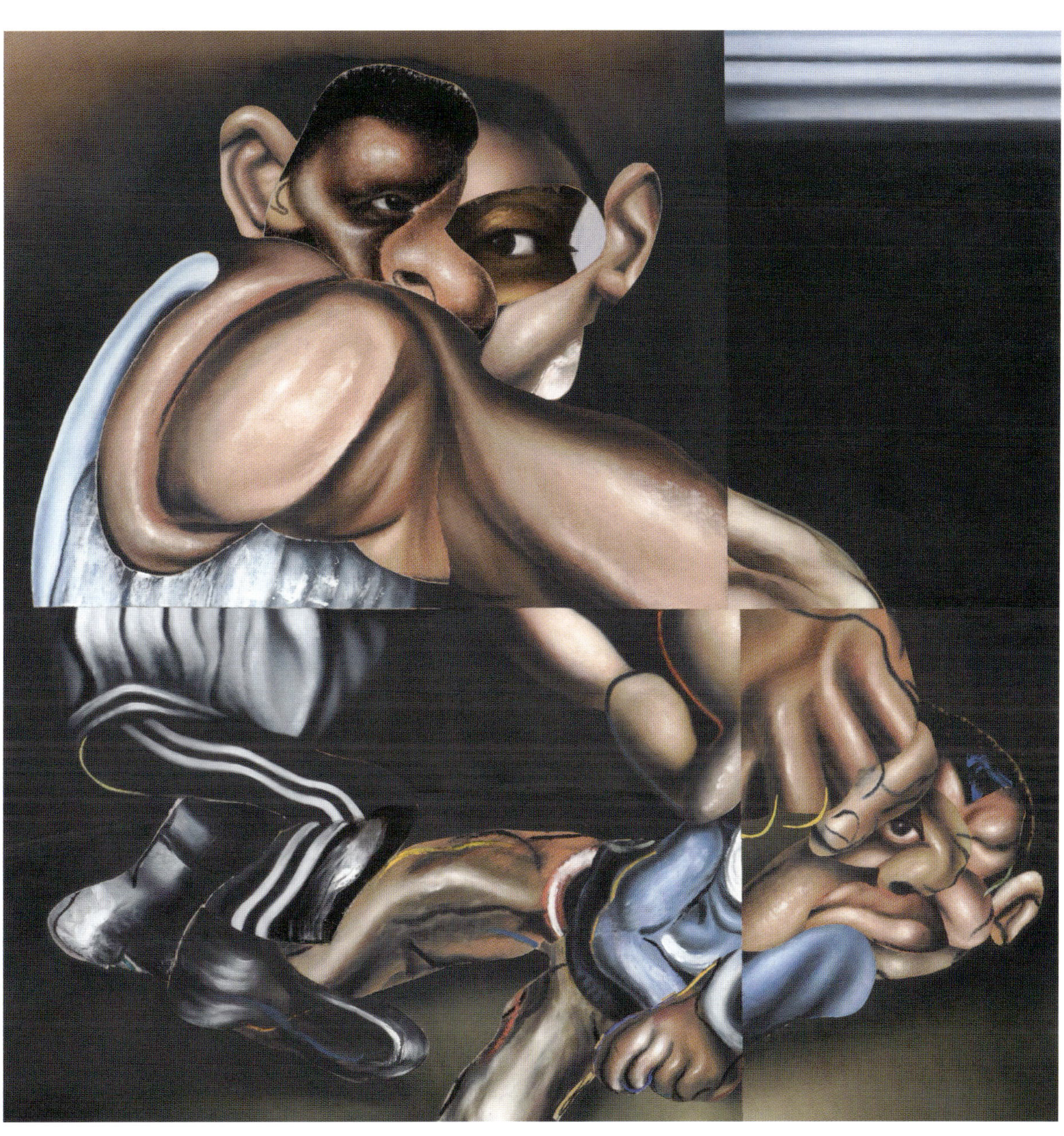

Punch-Out
2023
oil paint, oil pastel, gouache,
soft pastel, black charcoal
on linen canvas stretched
over wood panel
121.9 × 121.9 cm
Courtesy the Artist and Gagosian

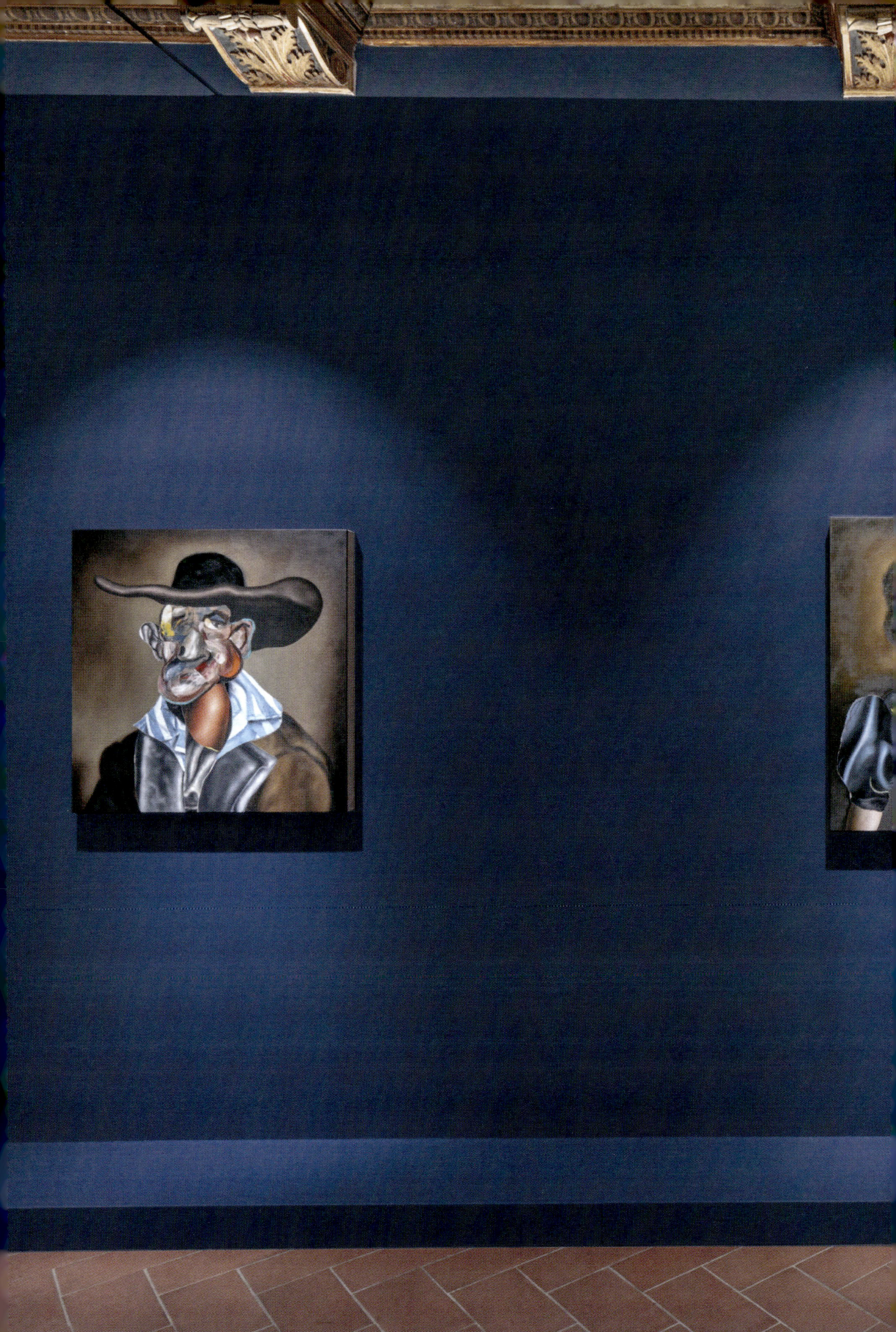

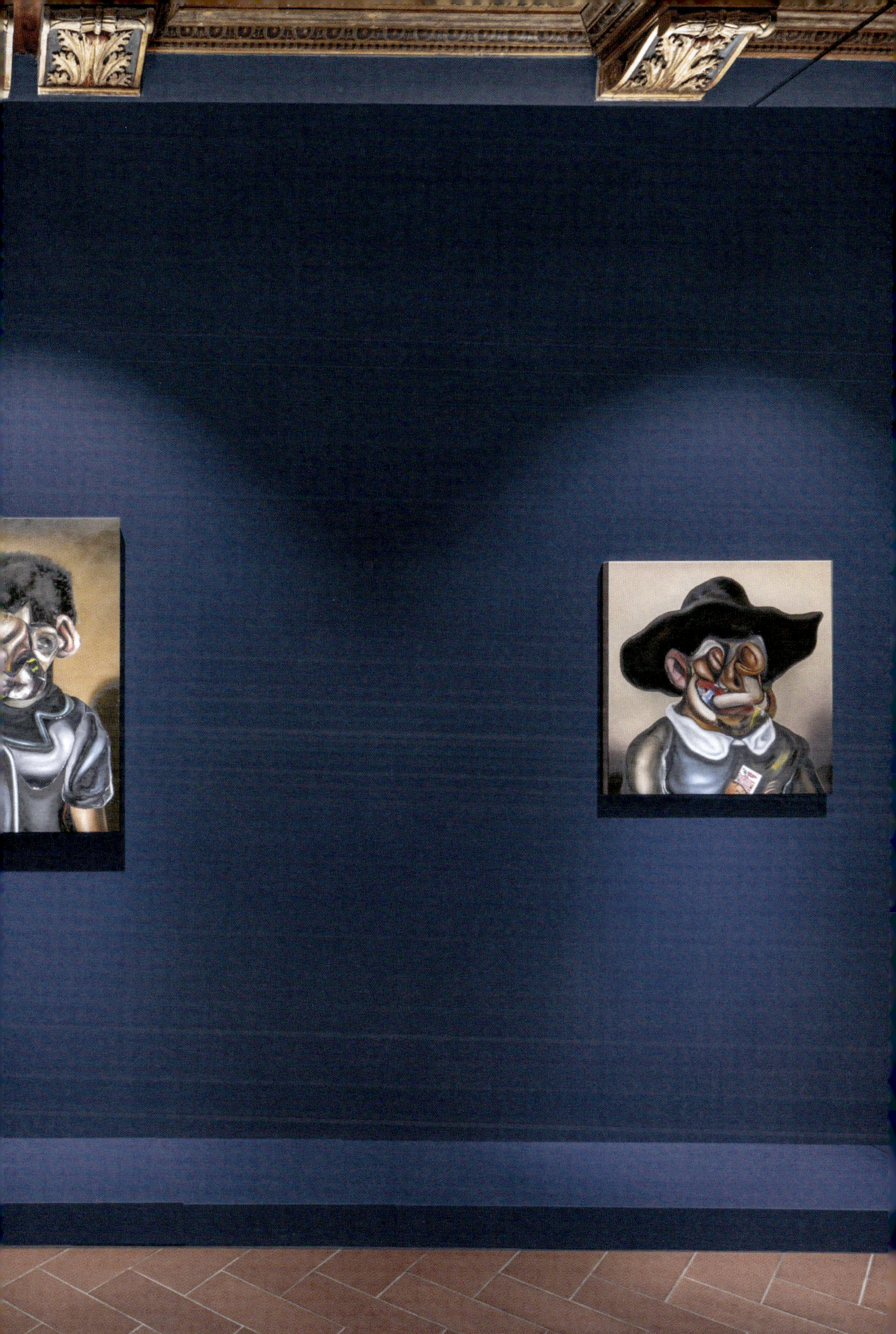

Mr. Shaw
2023
oil paint, oil pastel,
soft pastel, gouache,
black charcoal on linen canvas
stretched over wood panel
91.4 × 91.4 cm
Courtesy the Artist and Gagosian

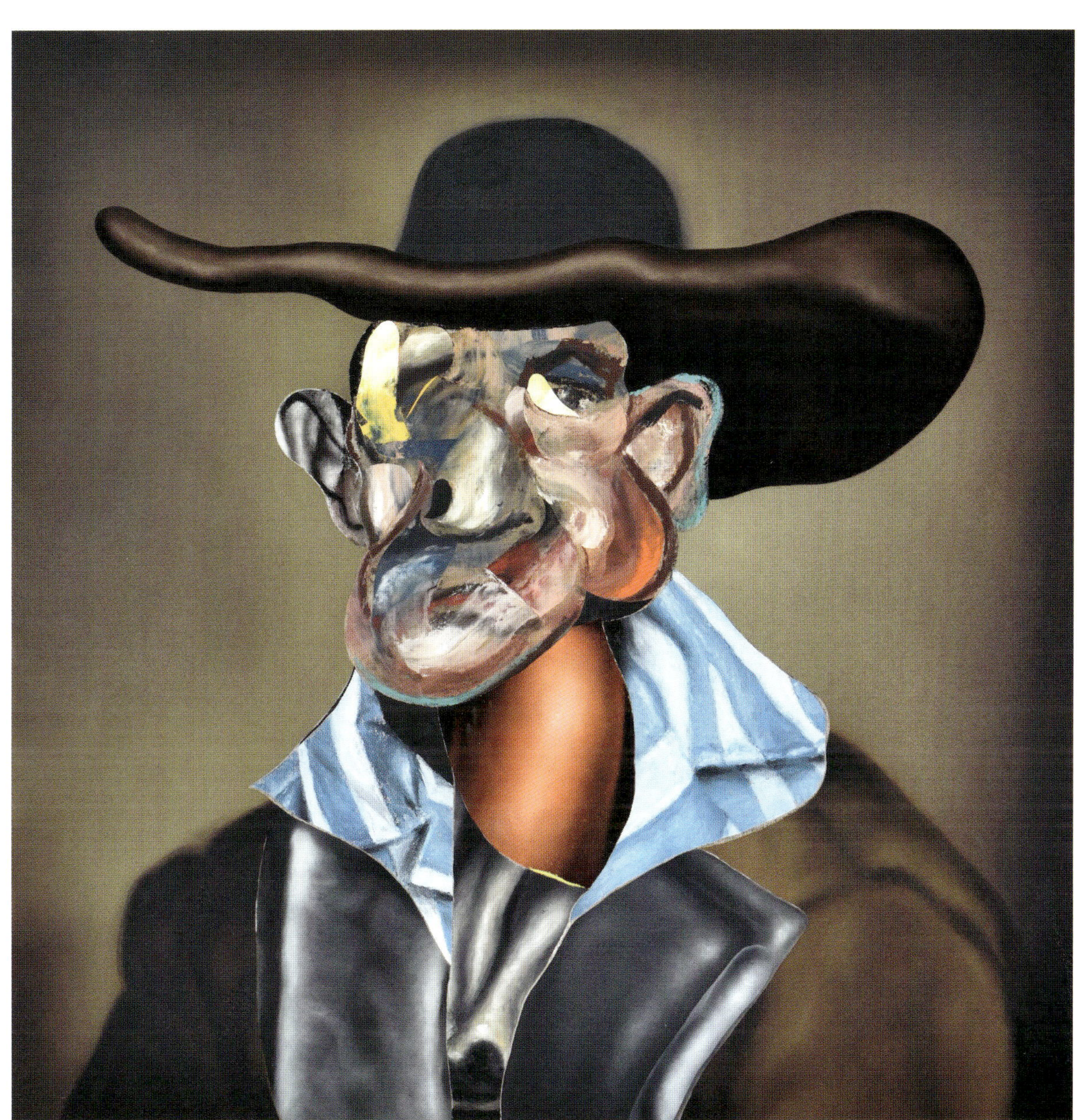

The Marcher
2023
oil paint, oil pastel,
gouache on linen canvas
stretched over wood panel
101.6 × 76.2 cm
Courtesy the Artist and Gagosian

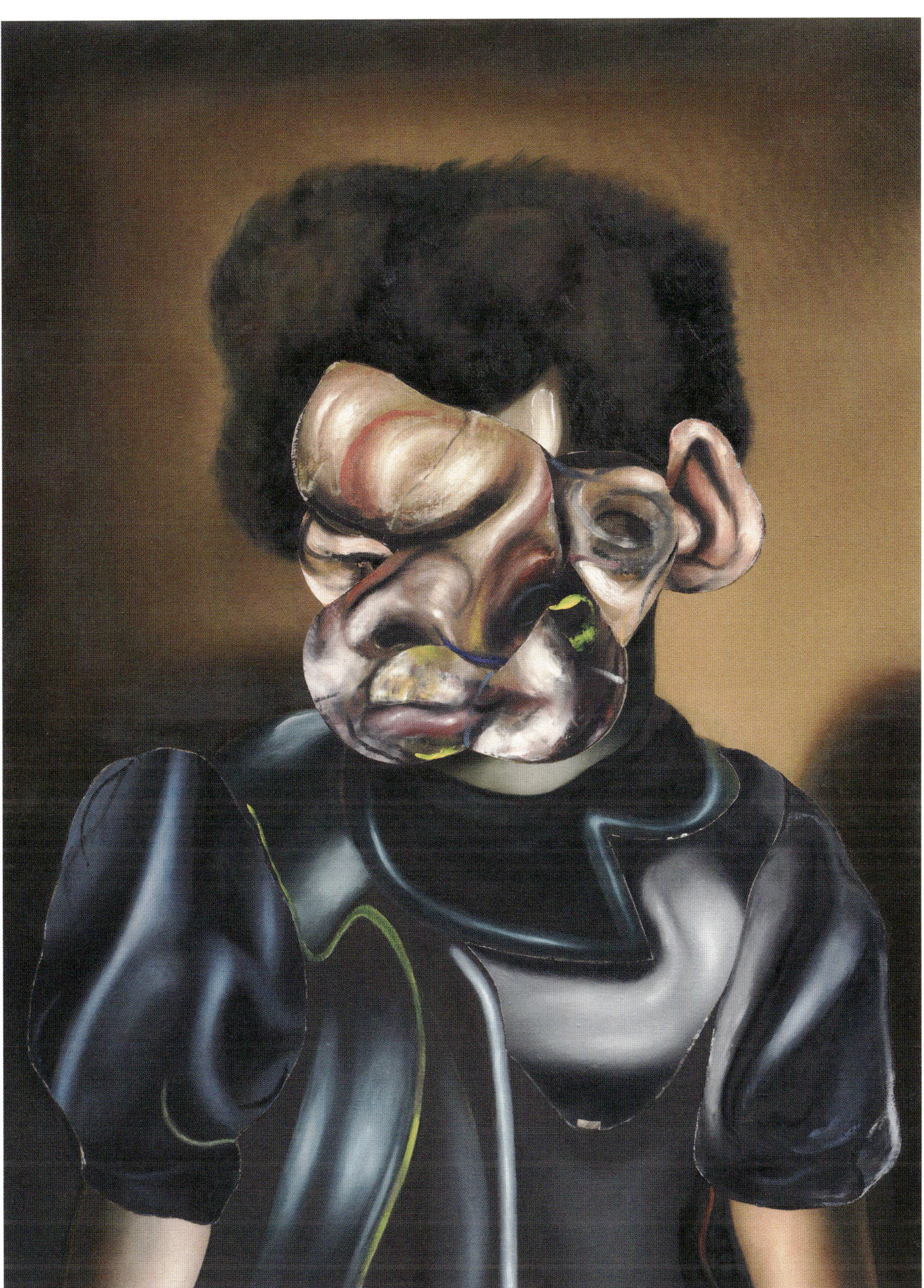

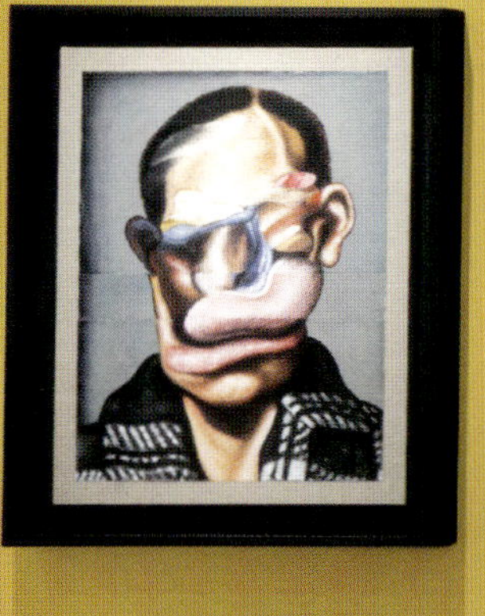

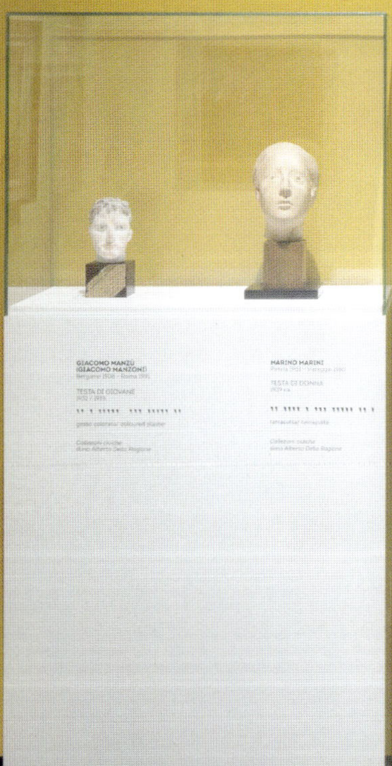

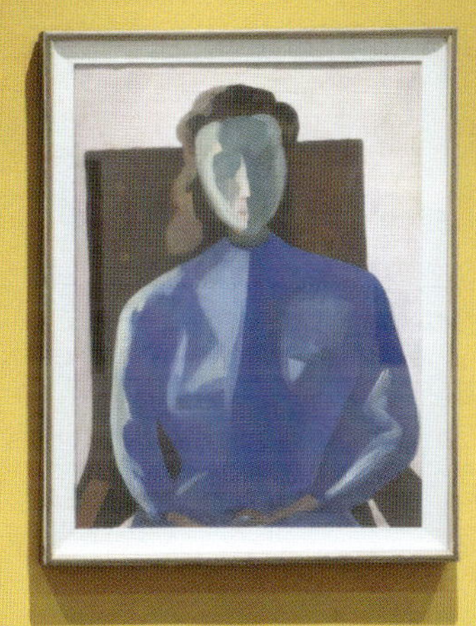

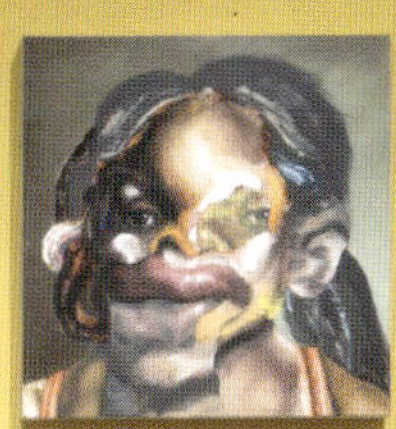

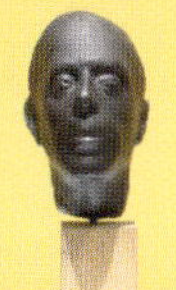
MARINO MARINI

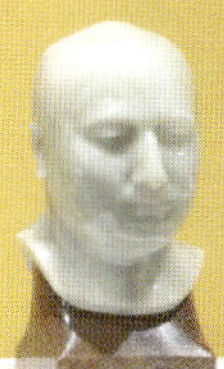
ANTONIETTA RAPHAËL
(ANTOINETTE DE SIMON RAPHAËL)

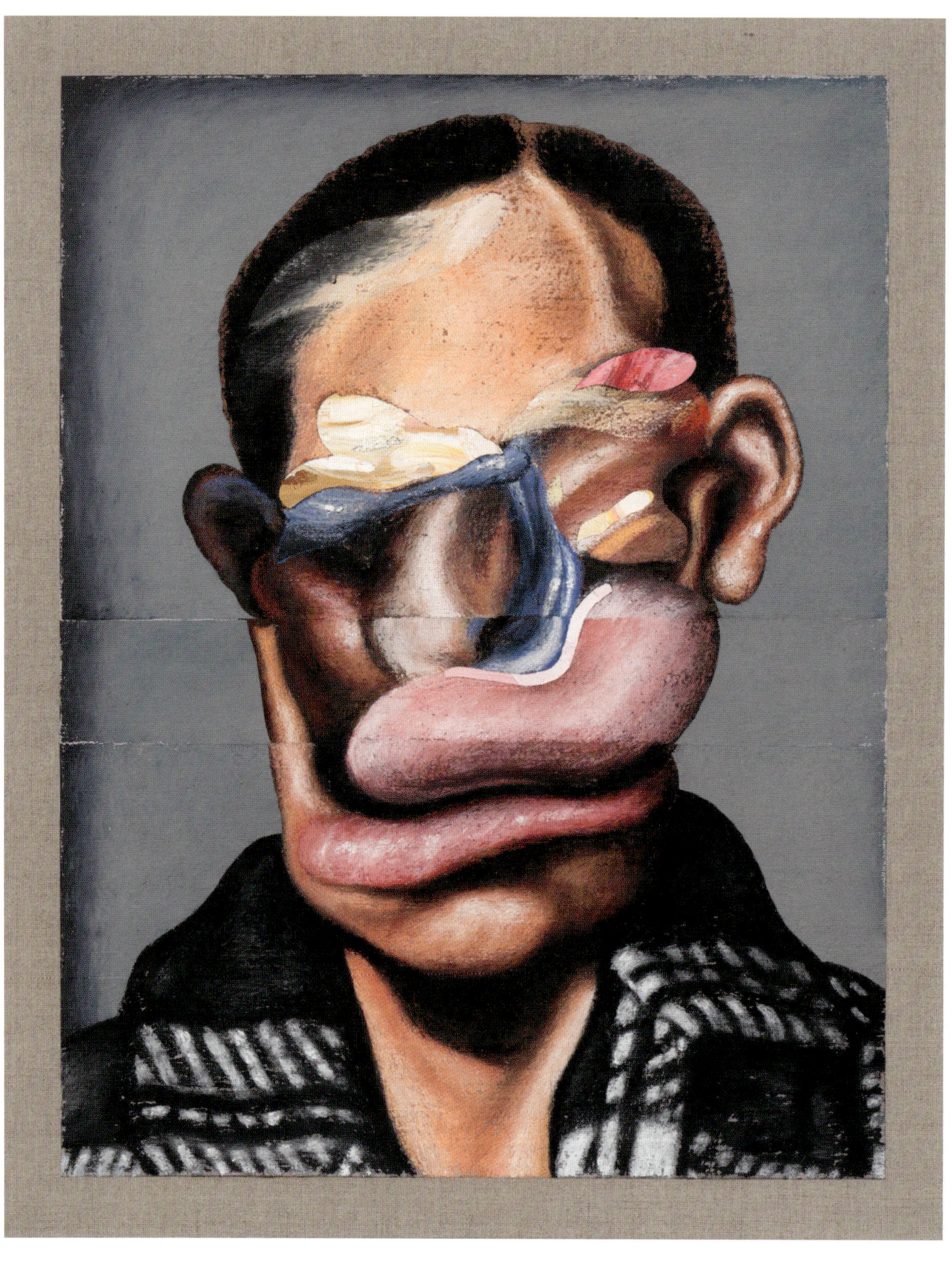

Doing Laundry
2019
oil paint, paint stick, gouache,
soft pastel on linen canvas
76.2 × 6 cm
Private collection

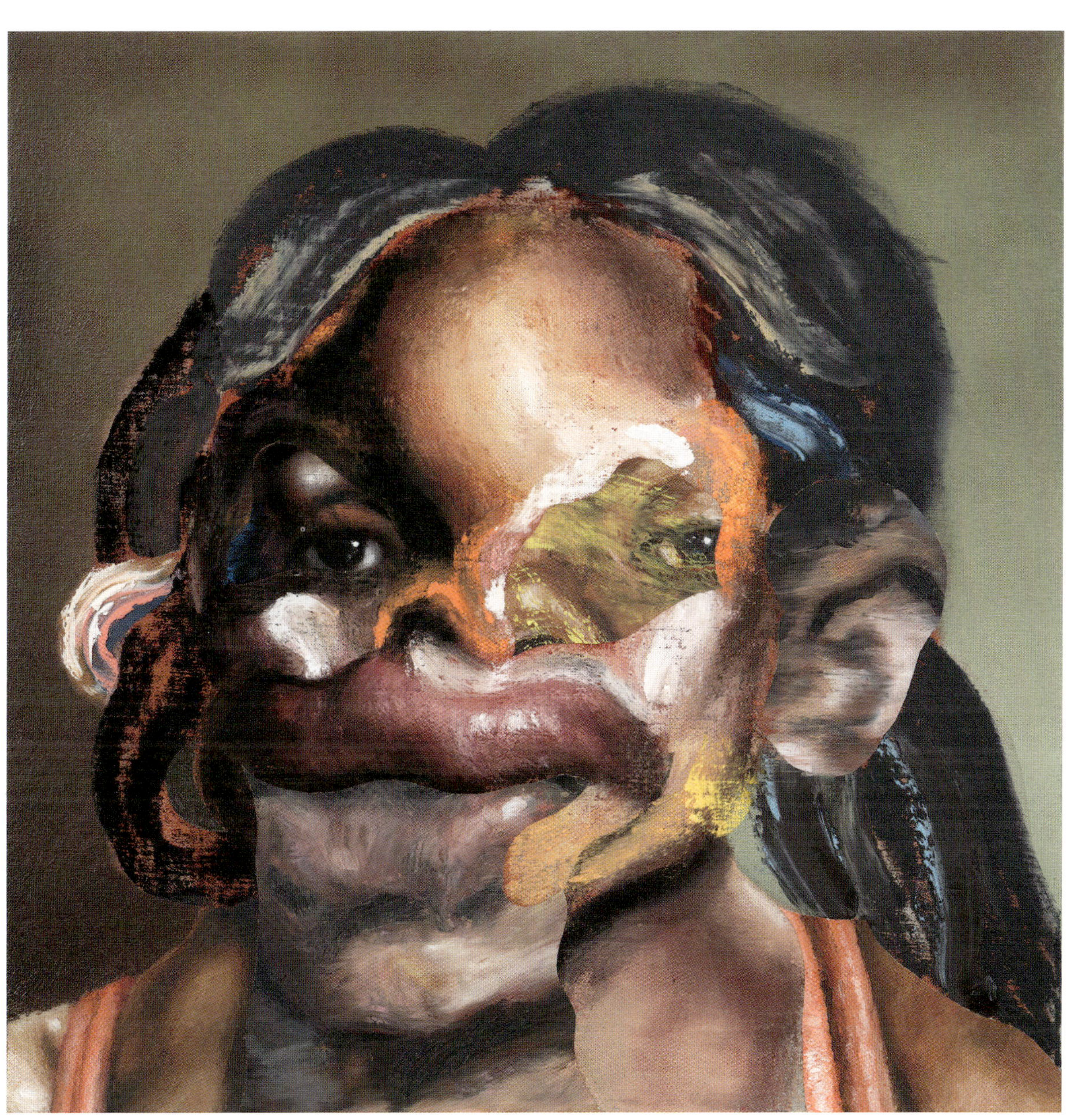

If It Wasn't For That Hospital Visit,
We Would Still Be Friends
2021
oil paint, paint stick, oil pastel,
soft pastel, gouache, black
charcoal on linen canvas
stretched over wood panel
50.8 × 50.8 cm
Collection Fredriksen Family Trust,
Norway

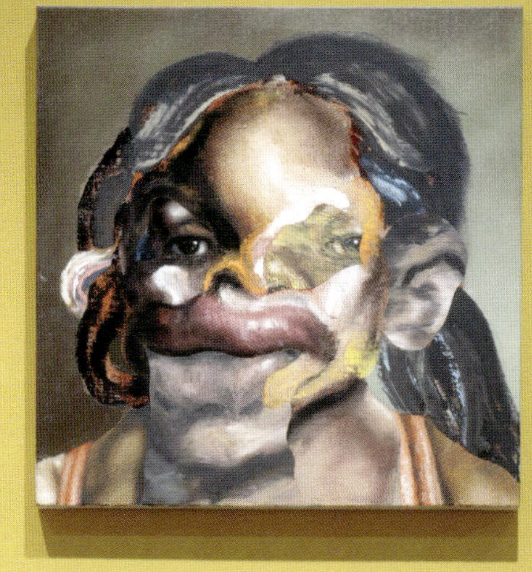

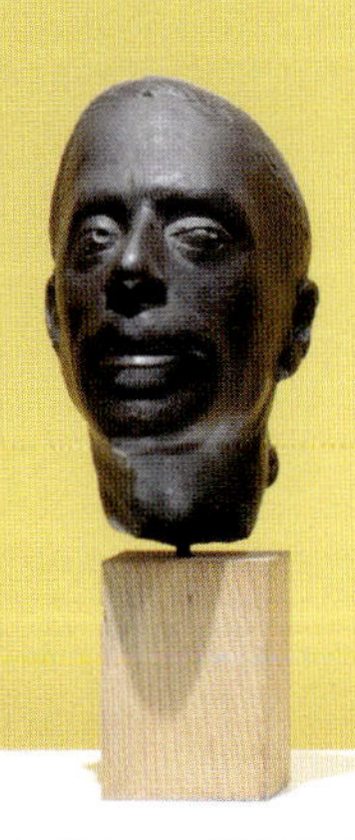
MARINO MARINI
Pistoia 1901 – Viareggio 1980
RITRATTO DI LAMBERTO VITALI
1936 - 1937 ca.
gesso, cera colorata/
plaster, coloured wax
Collezioni civiche,
dono Alberto Della Ragione

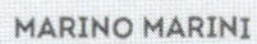

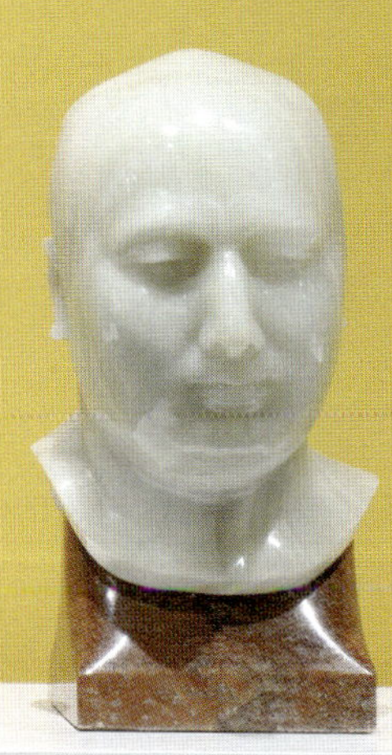
ANTONIETTA RAPHAËL
(ANTOINETTE DE SIMON RAPH.
Kaunas 1895 - Roma 1975
RITRATTO DI EMILIO JESI
1940
onice/ onyx
Collezioni civiche
dono Alberto Della Ragione

NATHANIEL MARY QUINN

Split Face

edited by
Sergio Risaliti
and
Stefania Rispoli

SilvanaEditoriale

Nathaniel Mary Quinn in the collections of Museo del Novecento and the Museo Stefano Bardini

Sergio Risaliti

The Museo Bardini is known around the world for its distinctive *mise-en-scène* of the antiquarian collection that belonged to Stefano Bardini, a prominent Florentine art dealer and collector at the turn of the twentieth century. An eclectic and extremely tasteful spirit prevails in the museum's highly atmospheric rooms, where valuable objects are positioned in a historicist reconstruction that embraces a varied set of major and minor arts relating to antiquity, the Middle Ages and the Renaissance. The museum features masterpieces from different ages, such as Tino da Camaino's *Charity* and Donatello's *Madonna dei Cordai*, in addition to paintings of extraordinary quality such as the monumental painted *Crucifix* of Bernardo Daddi, *Saint Michael Archangel* by Pollaiolo, *Night, Aurora and a Cupid* by Giovanni da San Giovanni and *Atlas* by Giovanni Francesco Barbieri known as Guercino. The treasure trove of a museum also contains a series of drawings by Giambattista Tiepolo and his sons Lorenzo and Domenico, together with others by Piazzetta, plus sublime figurative works in polychrome terracotta, a sizeable collection of rugs and arms, and furniture from different epochs. This museum-gallery has enthralled some of the most sensitive and sophisticated contemporary artists, especially those who, by studying and admiring the great art it houses, are able to reinterpret images and techniques with experimental boldness, embodying a notion of the avant-garde far removed from a sterile, melancholic and academic mannerism.

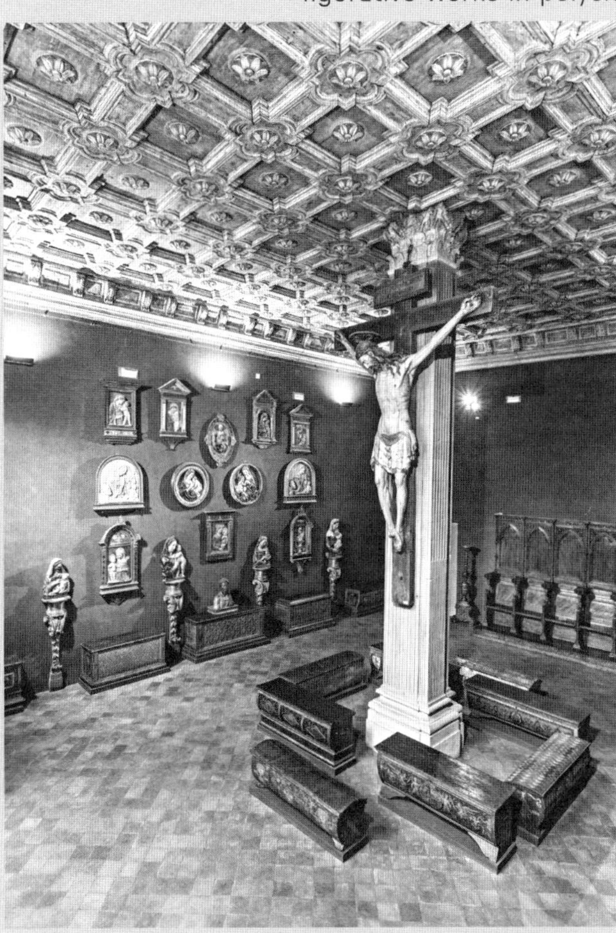

1. Sala delle Madonne, Museo Stefano Bardini, Florence

Among the many portraits produced by Nathaniel Mary Quinn and hung in the large hall of paintings in the Museo Stefano Bardini, there is one inspired by a portrayal of Duke Alessandro de' Medici known as Il Moro (Florence, 22 July 1510 – 6 January 1537) by Pontormo, who depicted the arrogant and dissolute ruler of Florence in the 1530s, that is, in the years after the collapse of the Florentine Republic with the return of the city's most powerful family at the time. Il Moro, so named due to his dark complexion, was the natural child of the pope's brother, Lorenzo, duke of Urbino and a Moorish servant, though he is believed by some to have actually been the son of the pope himself, who interceded with the emperor to have him appointed as the duke of Florence. Chronicles from the time describe him as a quintessentially violent tyrant, entirely without qualms and capable of any form of oppression, injustice and abuse of power. Alessandro's rule over the city was short-lived, because he was assassinated by his cousin in wild circumstances on the night between 6 and 7 January 1537. With his demise, the main line of the Medici family died out, but their power was soon

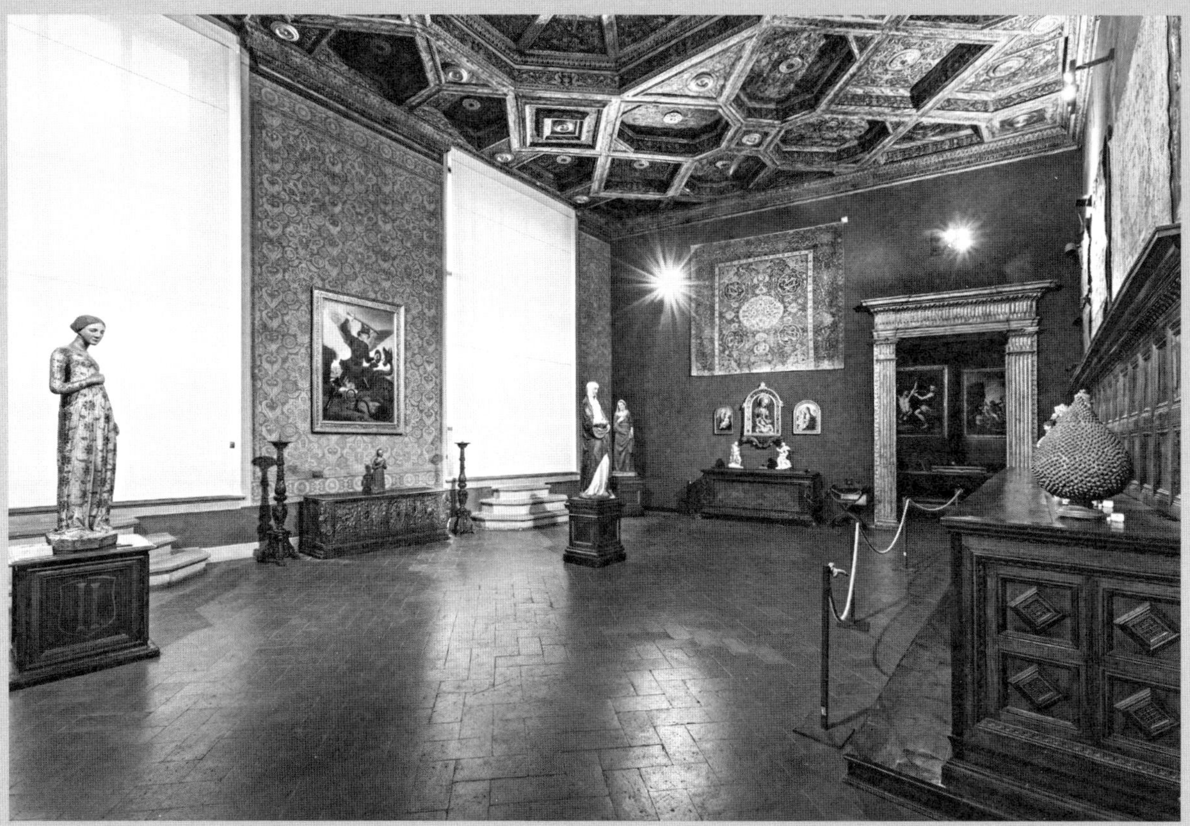

2. Sala del Terrazzo, Museo Stefano Bardini, Florence

reasserted with the ascent of Cosimo I from the "Popolano" branch. One of the many people who could not bear Alessandro and his overweening power was Michelangelo Buonarroti, who in a private letter referred to him as a "mule."

Like the Museo Bardini, the permanent collection of the Museo Novecento also came into being due to the foresight and love for visual culture of a courageous patron, Alberto Della Ragione. He began to devote himself to art at the end of the 1920s, when, still sceptical of what was being produced at the time, he purchased his first nineteenth-century works. His interest in twentieth-century art was finally sealed by a visit to the Quadriennale in Rome in 1931. Responding to an ethical call "not to move around the art of his age with [his] eyes closed, but to give the work of living artists the legitimate comfort of timely understanding," he began to lend his support to young artists often ignored by the art market and the critical establishment of the fascist regime. His collection of contemporary art grew gradually from then on and by the 1940s was already one of the largest in Italy. Della Ragione focused chiefly though not exclusively on figuration and a narrative fabric respectful of iconographic canons and genre, following the course of movements and currents such as Valori Plastici, Novecento, Magic Realism and Corrente. The works he collected included a substantial series of painted and sculptural portraits or, more generically, faces.

Awareness of one's image and the need to remember and be remembered are intertwined in portraiture, the origins of which were symbolically traced by Pliny the Elder to the silhouette a young maid produced of her lover to preserve an image of him as a memento while he was away. At the beginning of the twentieth century, with the *dis-integration* of the individual and the growing use of photography, portraiture became receptive to new representations of the human figure, focusing for the most part on anti-naturalistic renderings or on conveying an identity distinct from the one seen in the mirror. In the interwar years, many artists felt a need to revive tradition and to stick closely to the model, seeking to capture lines, expressions and gestures, starting with a modern and anti-monumental reworking of antiquity. This resulted, for example, in an intense contrast between the refined idealism of portraits by Antonietta Raphael and Marino Marini and the unadorned naturalism of Giacomo Manzù. Likewise, the rough and archaic painting of Massimo Campigli coexisted with the warm tones and constructive brushstrokes of Mario Mafai and Francesco Menzio, and with the synthetic painting of Virgilio Guidi and the Novecento-style purism of Pompeo Borra. Experimenting with different ways of painting—of treating the pictorial matter, combining and mixing colors—the painter discovered the innermost personality of the subject, which seems to emerge in the very process of painting.

In recent years, starting in 2018, we have regarded it as very important to engage with contemporary artists who explore portraiture with an intelligent and perceptive knowledge of how the genre evolved in previous centuries and with a bold, sometimes ironic and very personal inventiveness. In this regard I would like to mention John Currin, Glenn Brown, Y. Z. Kami and Jenny Saville, among others, who have all forged their own artistic vision encapsulated in the representation of the self, and who preceded Nathaniel Mary Quinn, whose wonderful exhibition, *Split Face*, was held across the gallery spaces of the permanent collection of the Museo Novecento and those of the Museo Stefano Bardini. I would like to thank Nathaniel Mary Quinn once again for having accepted our invitation and for having taken up, with great generosity and commitment, the challenge of dialoguing with works that are so representative of the history of western art from the Renaissance through to the last century.

Nathaniel Mary Quinn Split Face

Sergio
Risaliti
and
Stefania
Rispoli

I like to think that my work reflects uninhibited harmonious diversity—at times fluid and seamless, at times grotesque and discordant—but, surely, an embrace of reality as it is and the pursuit of what is possible. Rather than being a "collage" mentality, it's an "expressionist cubism" mentality, where one is able to embrace the rainbow-like spectrum of humanity, and as such, reflect our internalized worlds as a people.
Nathaniel Mary Quinn

Born and raised in a working-class suburb on Chicago's South Side, Nathaniel Mary Quinn (1977) began drawing at the age of five. He moved to Indiana when he was very young to study at Culver Academies on a scholarship, later graduating in art and psychology at Wabash College in Crawfordsville (Indiana) and taking a further degree at New York University. His works can now be found in important public and private collections, including those of the Whitney Museum of American Art (New York), the MOCA (Los Angeles), the Brooklyn Museum (New York) and the Centre Pompidou (Paris).

Split Face, his first solo exhibition in Italy, opened in October 2023 and was divided between the Museo Novecento and the Museo Stefano Bardini in Florence. The show comprised a selection of previously unseen and recently produced works, which were hung among masterpieces of Florentine Renaissance portraiture and twentieth-century Italian art—from Donatello, Pollaiolo and the Della Robbia to Felice Casorati, Virgilio Guidi, Carlo Levi and many others—, creating a surprising and intense dialogue between different languages, times and visions. Since 2018, the theme of the face has frequently taken center stage in the exhibition programming of Museo Novecento, often in collaboration with other Florentine cultural institutions. This focus has been explored through exhibitions dedicated to artists such as Jenny Saville, John Currin, Glenn Brown, Y.Z. Kami, Medardo Rosso, and Robert Mapplethorpe. The face also constitutes one of the thematic sections of the museum's permanent collection display, reflecting the particular interest of patron Alberto Della Ragione in physiognomic representation and portraiture—understood as the artistic rendering of the inner worlds of individuals—through the diverse stylistic approaches that characterized early 20th-century Italian art.

Quinn's portraits appear to the eye as two-dimensional pictorial sculptures, layered compositions charged with visual tension that openly challenge traditional codes of representation to create an effect of disorientation. Colorful and grotesque, the images are the result of a meticulous process of construction and deconstruction, in which personal memories are combined with photographs, advertisements, prints and illustrations of various kinds drawn from an open archive accumulated over the years. Detached from their original context, these visual fragments are broken down and reassembled into new configurations, yielding deformed and disturbing, yet profoundly human, faces.

On the following pages
1. Legacy of Alberto Della Ragione, permanent collection at Museo Novecento, Florence

GIACOMO MANZÙ
(GIACOMO MANZONI)
TESTA DI GIOVANE
gesso colorato/ coloured plaster
Collezioni civiche

Nathaniel Mary Quinn Split Face

The same propensity for *pastiche* can be found in Quinn's use of painting techniques. Oils, gouache, pastels, charcoals, oil sticks and so on are juxtaposed in a discontinuous and constantly varying manner on the surface of his paintings. In his apparently chaotic compositions, he has in fact perfected an exceptional pictorial technique over the years, combining meticulous attention to detail with an aptitude for hyperrealism and cartooning that is perhaps reminiscent of some of the sophisticated visual manipulations produced by artificial intelligence. In constructing these pictorial assemblages, he proceeds by way of layering, treating each portion of the body as a form in its own right, distinct but at the same time equal to the others. He covers and uncovers segments of the canvas as he paints, with the result that the figures are created in pieces, in distinct phases, and are only revealed in their entirety at the end, as a truth that is discovered bit by bit. The faces therefore seem to be cut out and produced from images that are torn into pieces and then recombined so that they correspond, in line with the artist's intent, to the face of the sitter, or rather, to the perception or a particular feeling that the subject arouses. The final effect is an interplay of superimpositions between physical and ideal planes, which, in the two-dimensionality of the canvas, or paper support, reveal their own specific and distinct depth.

In his portraits Quinn fuses a biographical universe populated by real events, people and memories with a vast range of imagery that takes in both high and low culture, accumulating multiple levels of memory but above all exploring our capacity to process memories and to perceive the Other. In digging into and excavating from the meanders of the mind, the artist retraces the path that was paved by the great masters of the early twentieth century—from the deconstruction of Cubist collages to the experiments of the Surrealists, through to the introspective inquiries of artists like Bacon, Freud, Dumas and others—who had completely upended the canon of beauty that had dominated portraiture until the nineteenth century by promoting freedom of interpretation with regard to composition, balance and human psychology. No longer bound by academic constraints, the human figure became the site of constant metamorphosis, of a restless and multiple truth.

Drawing on sources of inspiration that also include music, literature and psychology, Quinn places the "cut and sew" montage experimented with by the avant-garde in both art and fashion at the center of his study of the human figure, around which his artistic practice revolves. The characters in works such as *The Executive Director* (2019), *After Pontormo's Portrait of Alessandro de' Medici* (2023), and *The Record Player* (2023) have none of the smoothness and formal correctness of certain contemporary images, still inclined to exploit classical and Renaissance forms through flat citations made in a postmodern spirit. Indeed, they are stretched, collapsing and distorted figures made up of a seductive formal *cocktail* that can be brutal at times. This process of elaborating forms invites reflection on how we perceive reality

On the following pages
2. Inside the Museo Stefano Bardini, Florence

3. Sala dei Dipinti, Museo Stefano Bardini, Florence

as it unfolds, what we communicate about it, how we construct our public and private image and how much we invest in representing our lives and those of others.

Quinn pushes us to look not for resemblance but for revelation: each face is a constellation of possible identities, an inner map that disorients and questions.

If the portraiture of the past centered on the cult of the person and the rendering of a precise, powerful and idealized image of the subject, and if a certain use of social media induces us to embrace this model of representation, Quinn's portraits move in the opposite direction. Lying behind the visual power of his works is a profound social and cultural reflection that addresses issues of marginalization and resilience. The transfiguration of a face—from familiar to disturbing, from reassuring to violent and vice versa—is not just an aesthetic but also an existential act of reconstruction of the human figure in all its complexity. It is an attempt to give form to the invisible, to restore dignity and complexity to subjects that are often marginalized.

Looking at works such as *Mama, Joe, and James Brown* (2023) and *Mr. Nightmare* (2020) we are prompted to call into question the frequently saccharine models of perception with which we interpret the face of another person. In this sense, the *Split Face* exhibition, centering on a close juxtaposition between his works and those of the Museo Stefano Bardini and Museo Novecento collections, openly challenges the canons of beauty and harmony. More than on previous occasions—monographic exhibitions in the same spaces featuring artists such as John Currin, Glenn Brown, Luca Pignatelli, Anj Smith, Emiliano Maggi and Rachel Feinstein—the dialogue becomes controversial and the juxtaposition disorienting. His entrance into the historical rooms of the two museums is akin to that of a boxer bounding into the Botticelli room at the Uffizi, a genuine challenge to the balance of Renaissance painting, as were Picasso's cubist faces or Bacon's swollen, boneless figures. The presence of his paintings acquires the symbolic force of a temporal and cultural collision, like an "anti-graceful" painting, to cite Carlo Carrà, that bursts in among the smooth Renaissance forms and questions our ability to accept the complexity—including the most disturbing kind—of human identity.

In the way they interweave reality and fiction, memory and imagination, autobiography and society, Quinn's works remind us that every portrait is, first and foremost, an exercise of the gaze. And it is in this exercise—as visual as it is emotional—that the restless and contemporary force of his painting lies. In the Museo Bardini, among paintings, sculptures and objects of classical, medieval and Renaissance art, Quinn's canvases and works on paper shout out loud and reaffirm that they belong to the world of reality, between truth and appearance.

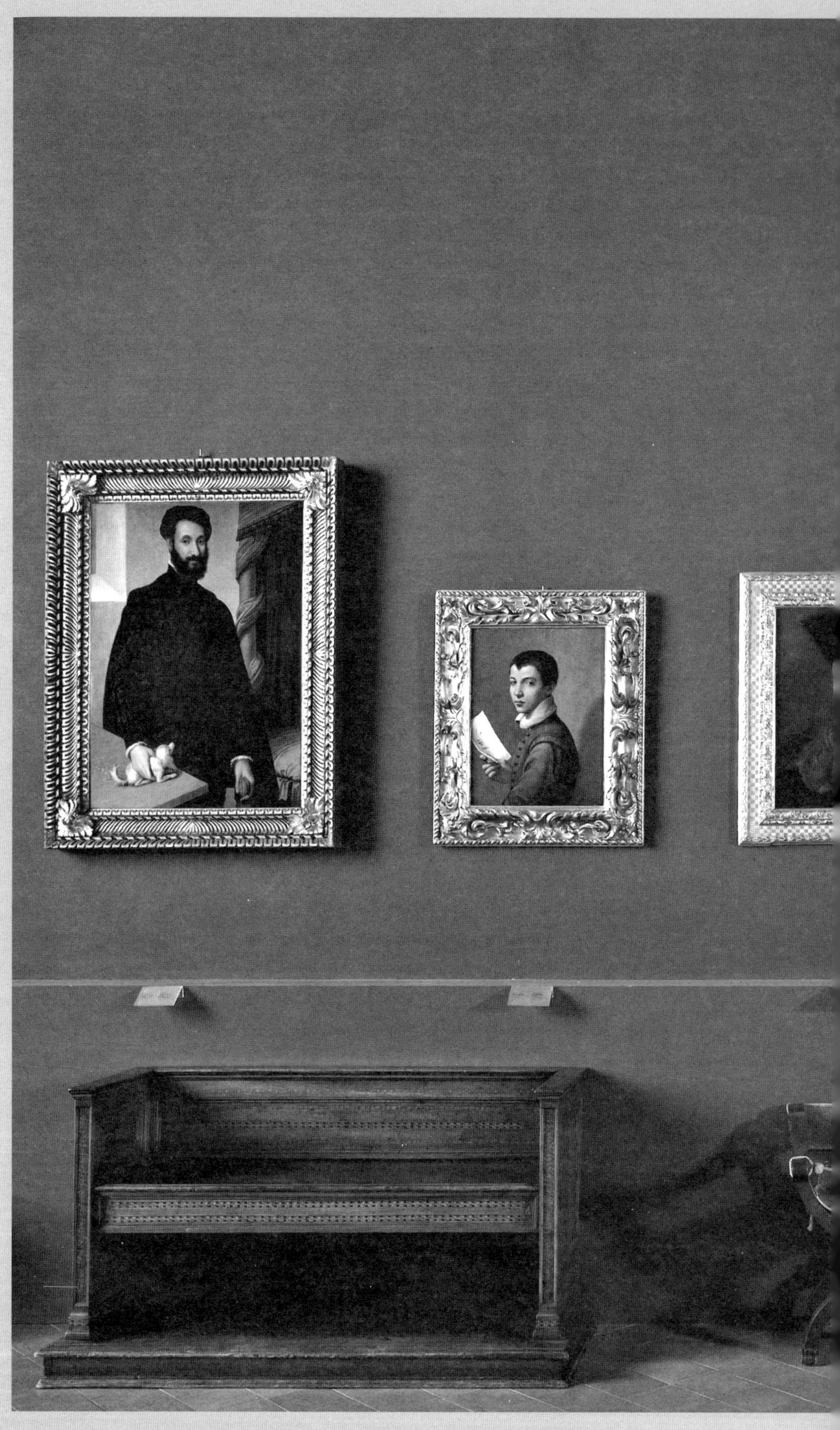

Sergio Risaliti and Stefania Rispoli

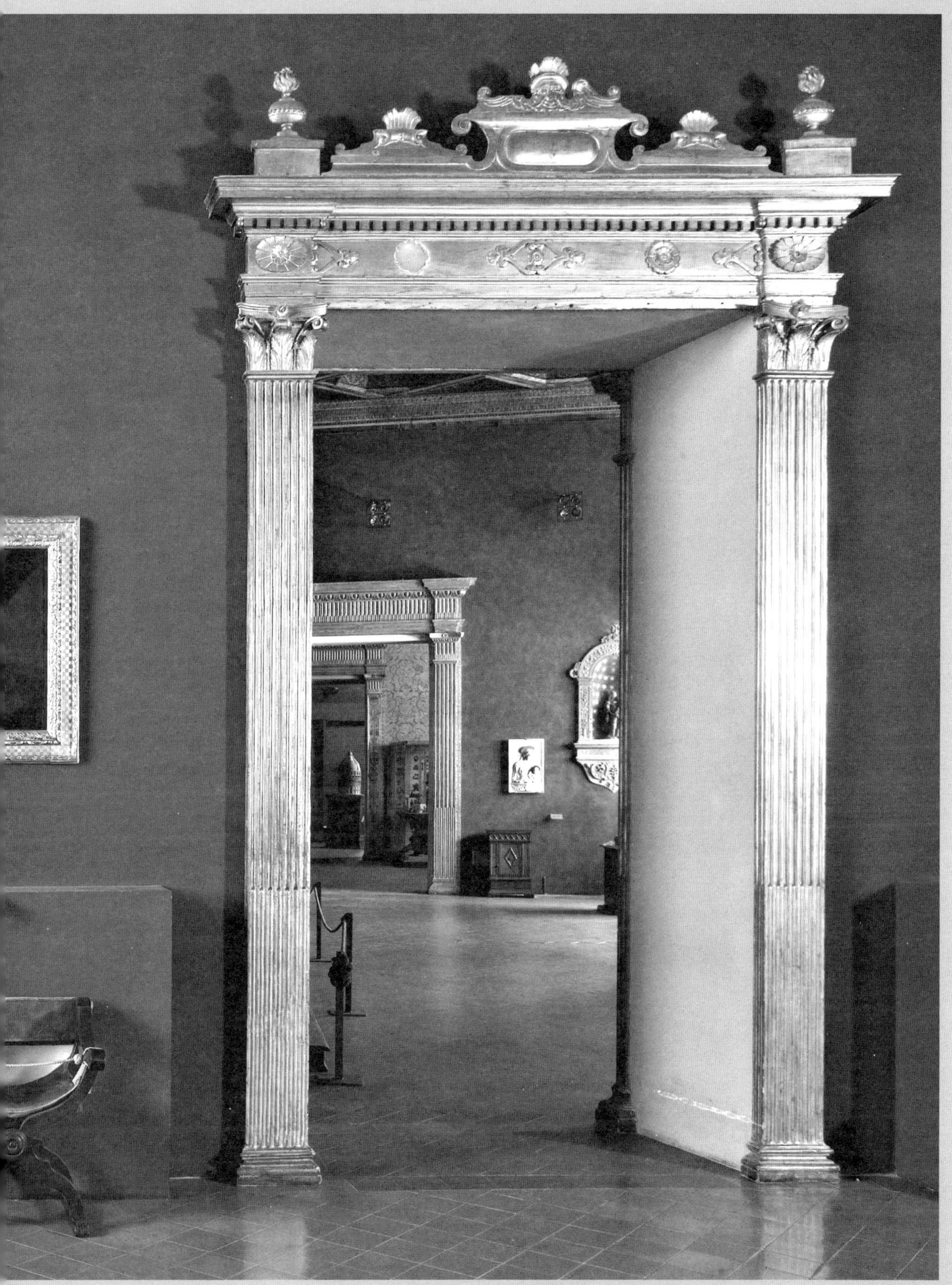

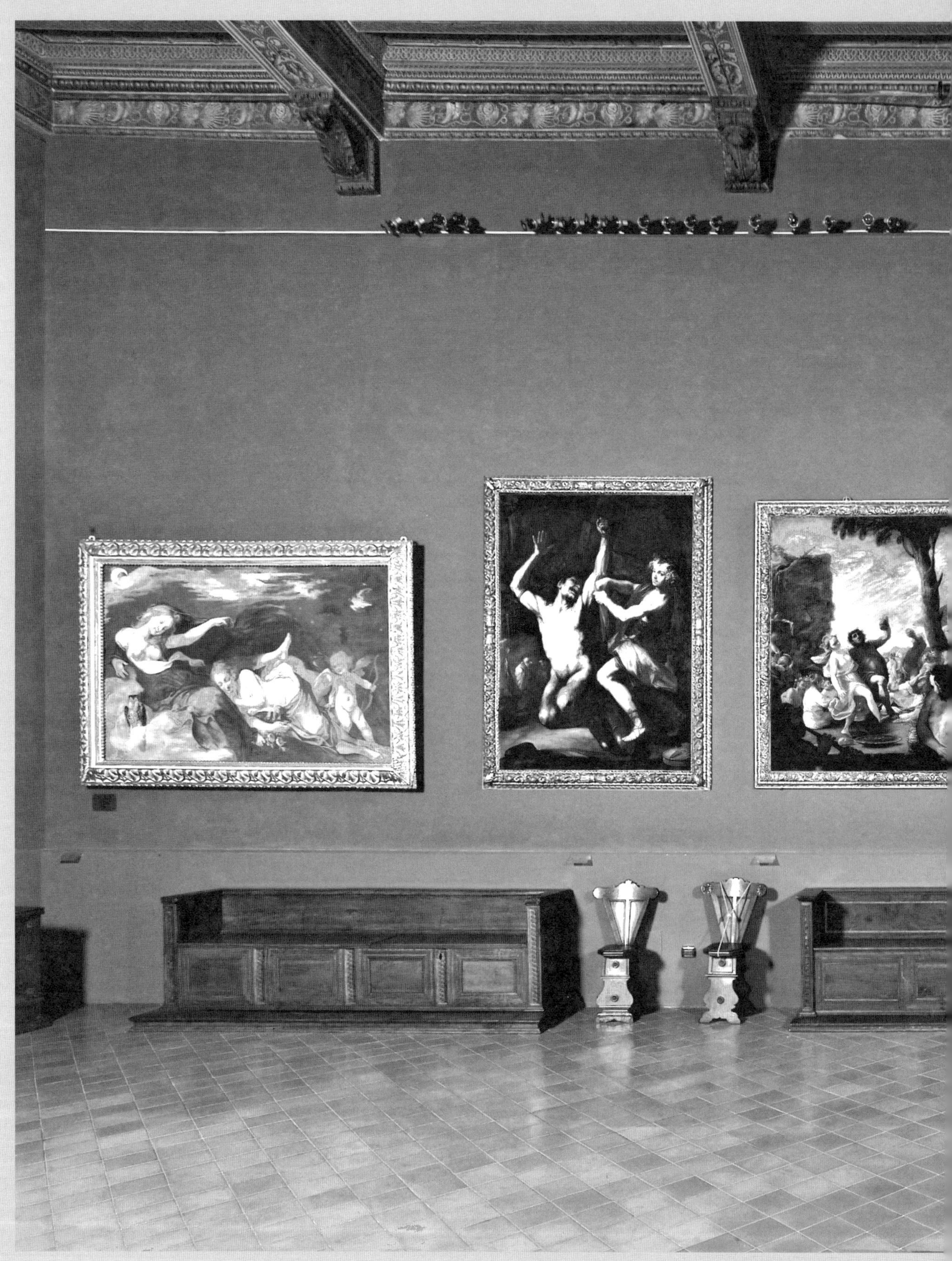

Sergio Risaliti and Stefania Rispoli

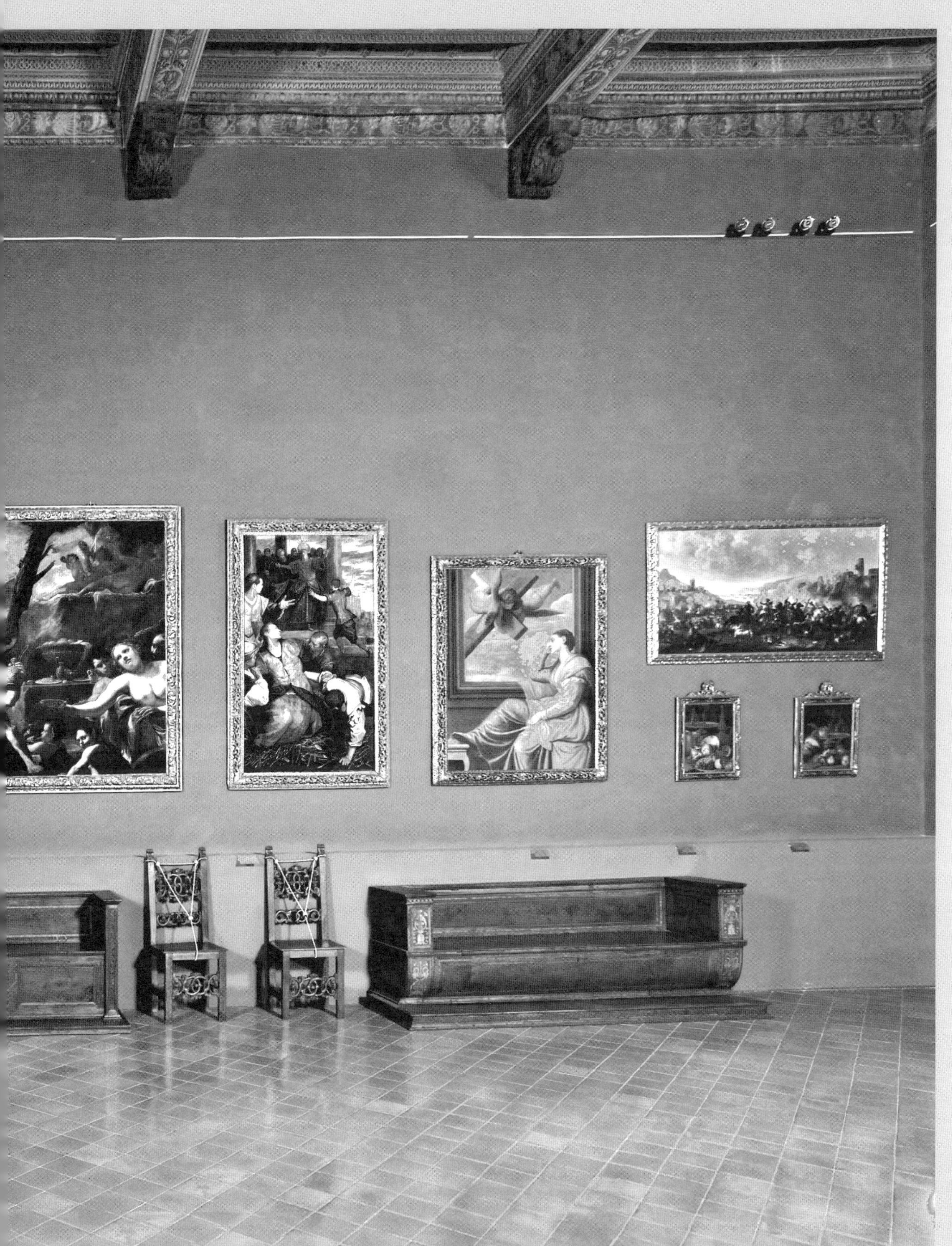

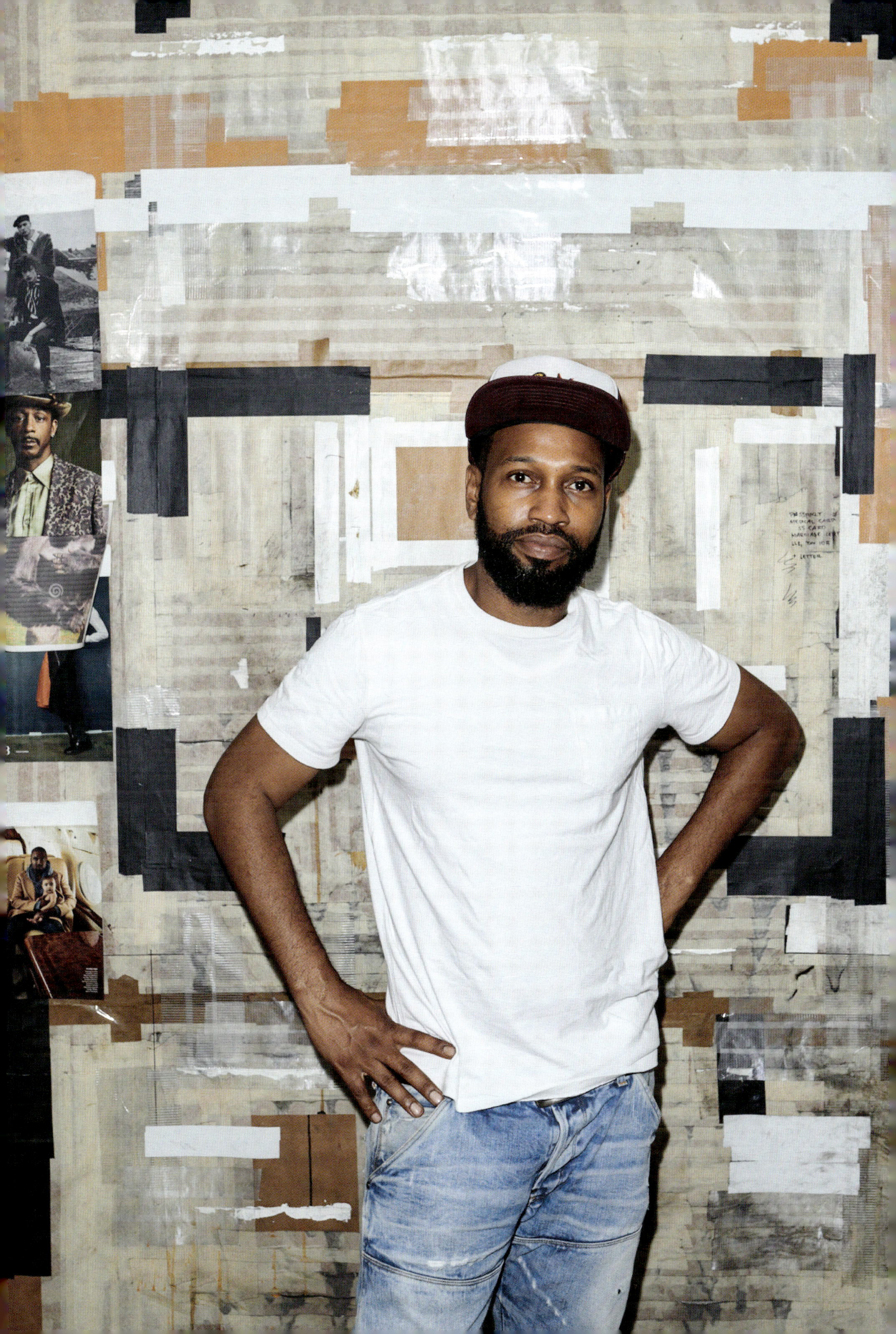

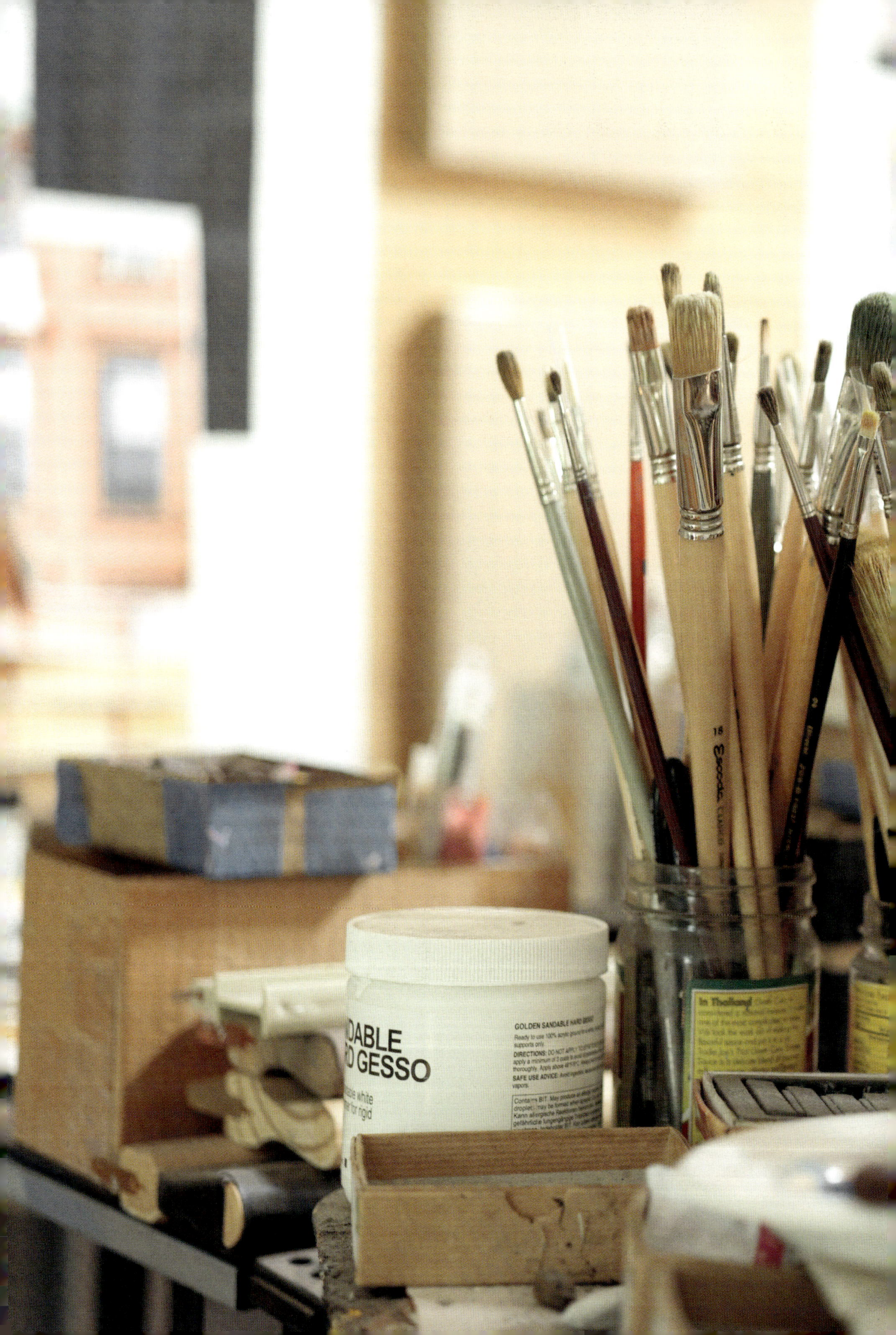
DABLE
D GESSO
GOLDEN SANDABLE HARD GESSO
In Thailand

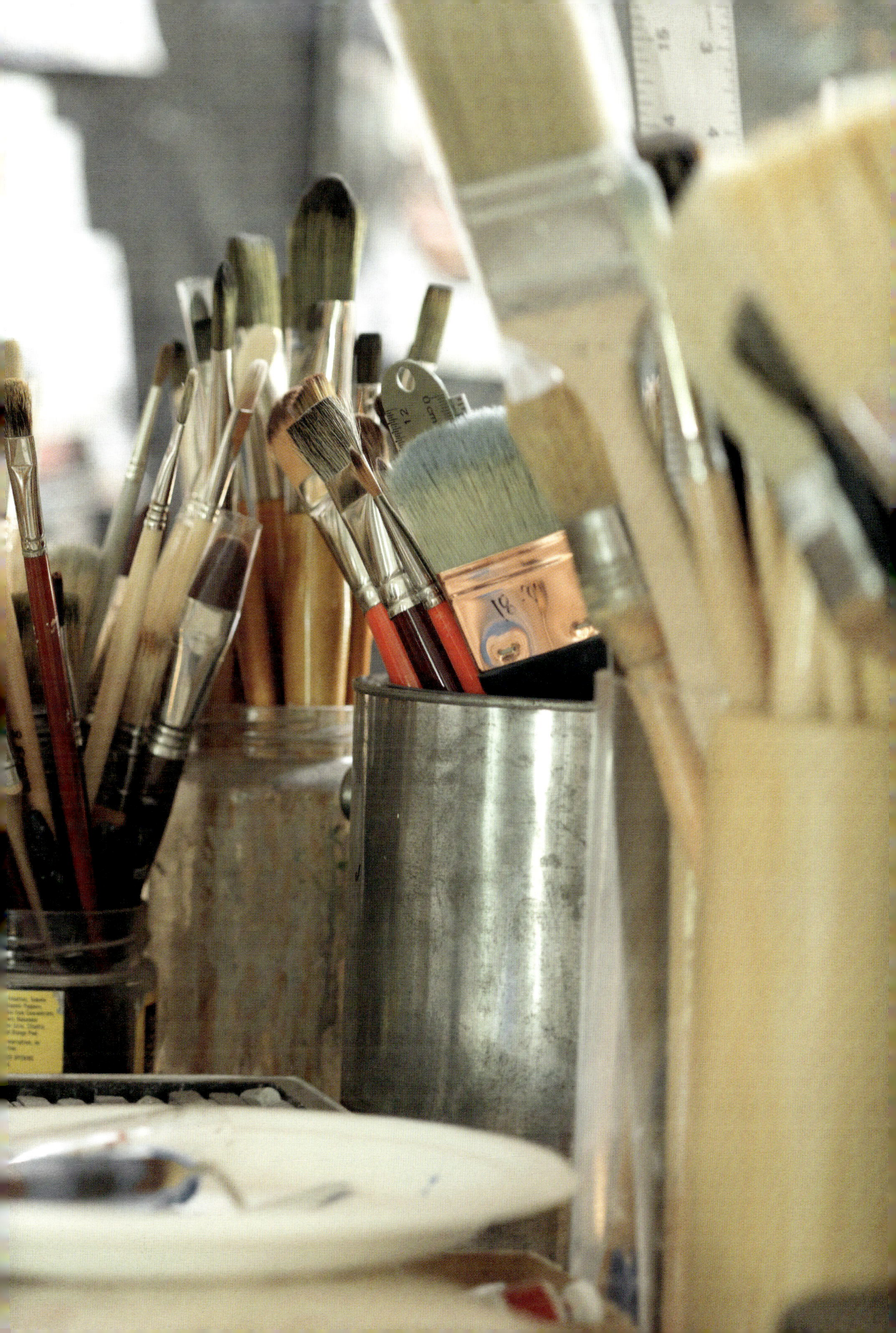

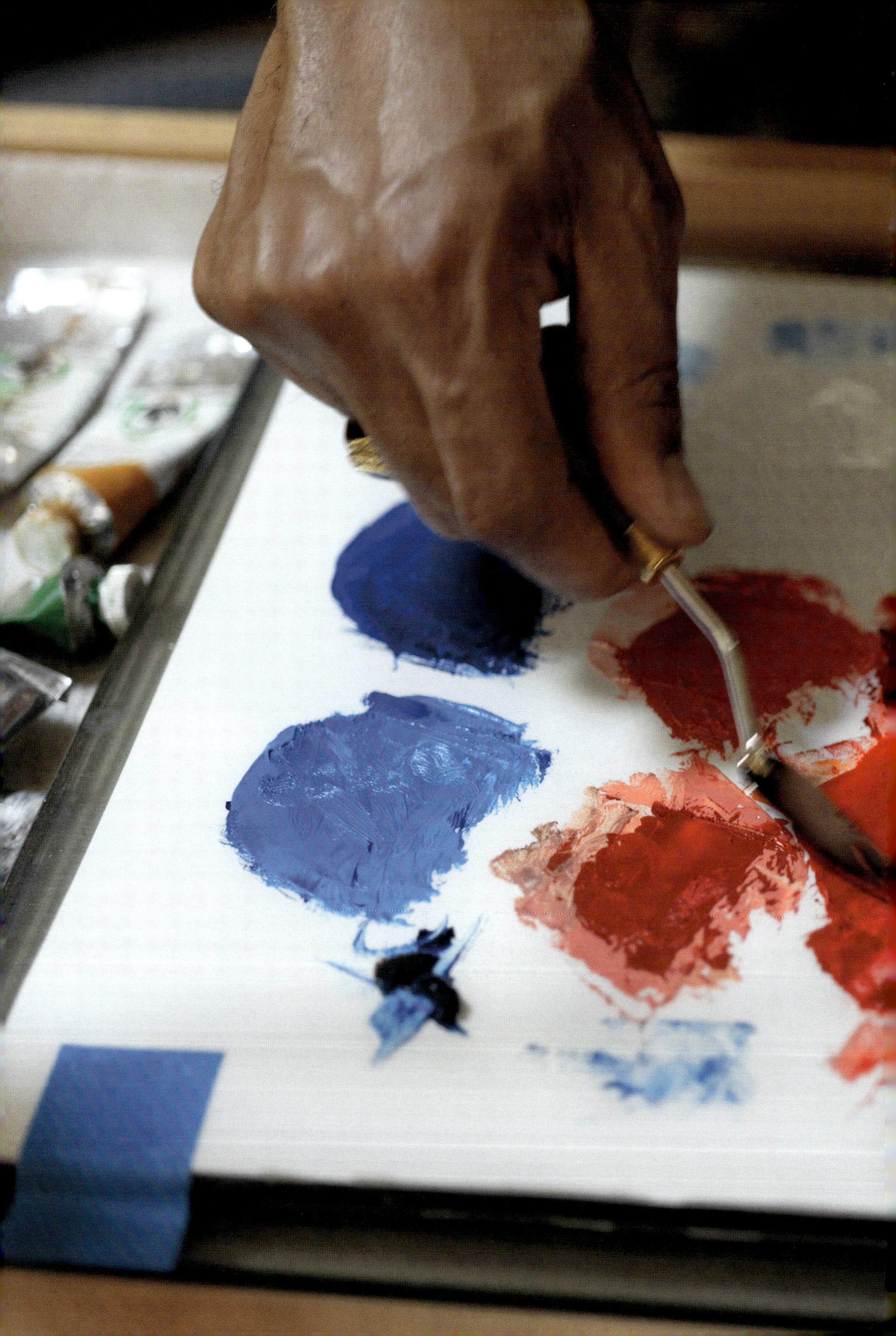

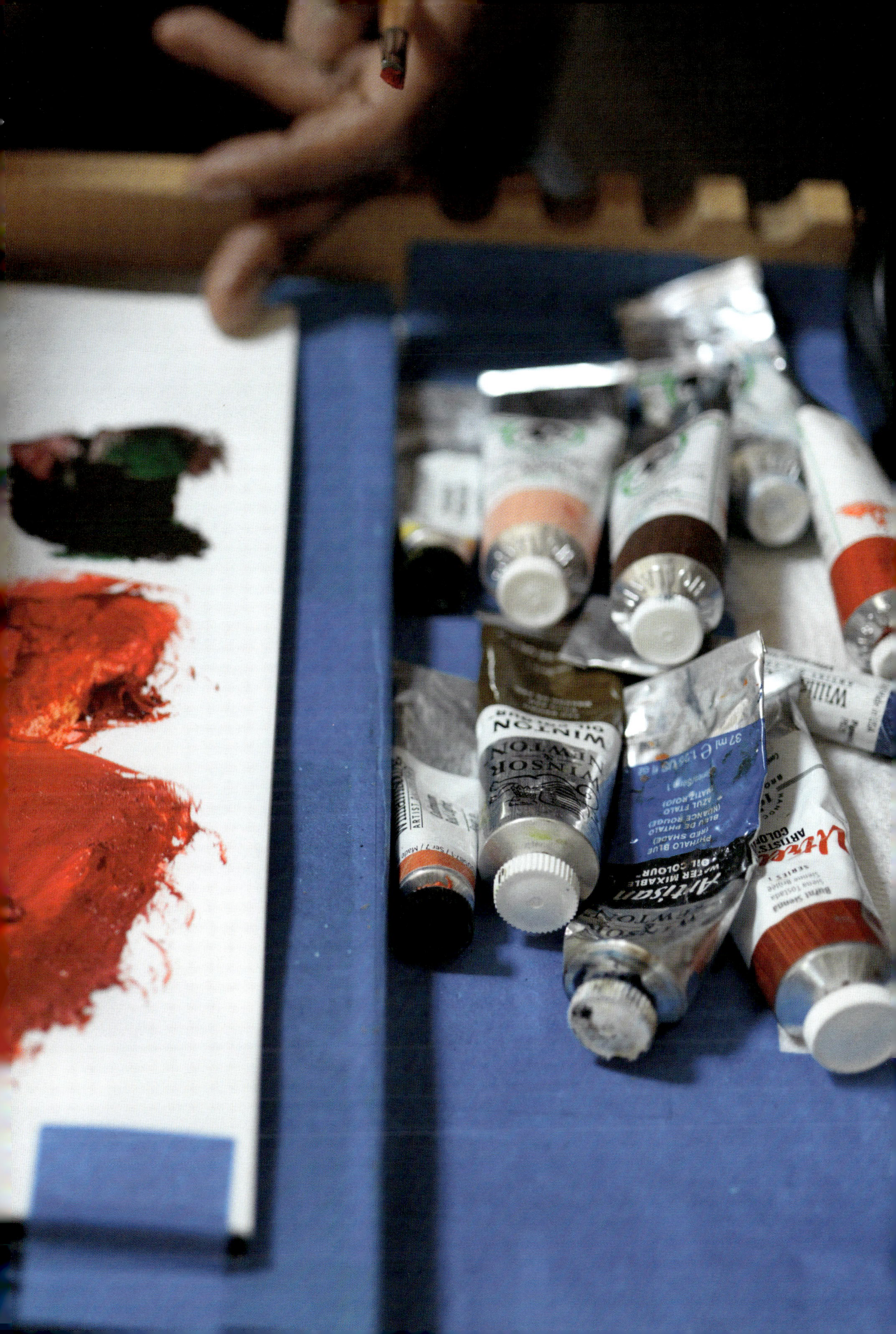
WINSOR & NEWTON
Artisan
WATER MIXABLE OIL COLOUR
PHTHALO BLUE (RED SHADE)
37 ml

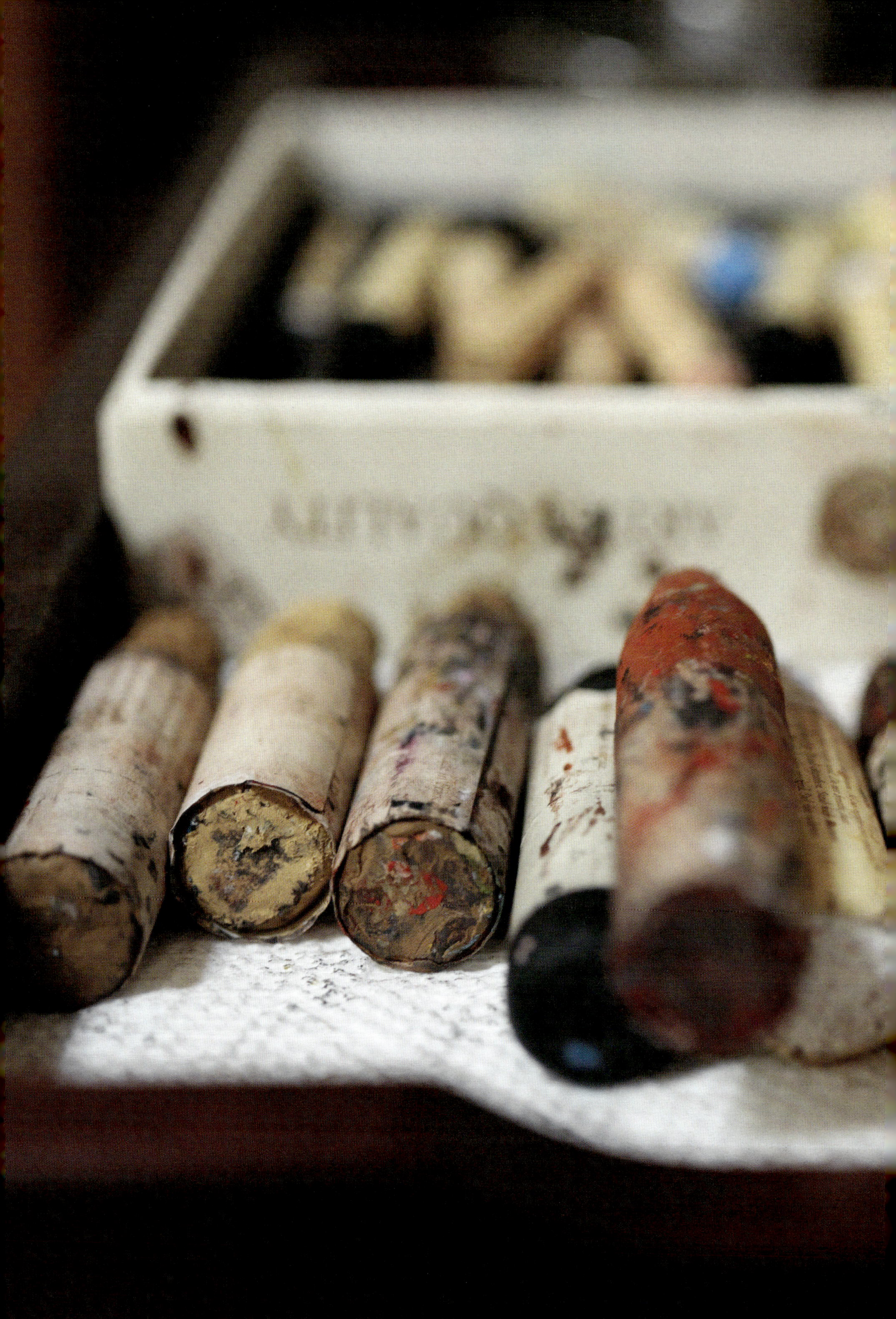

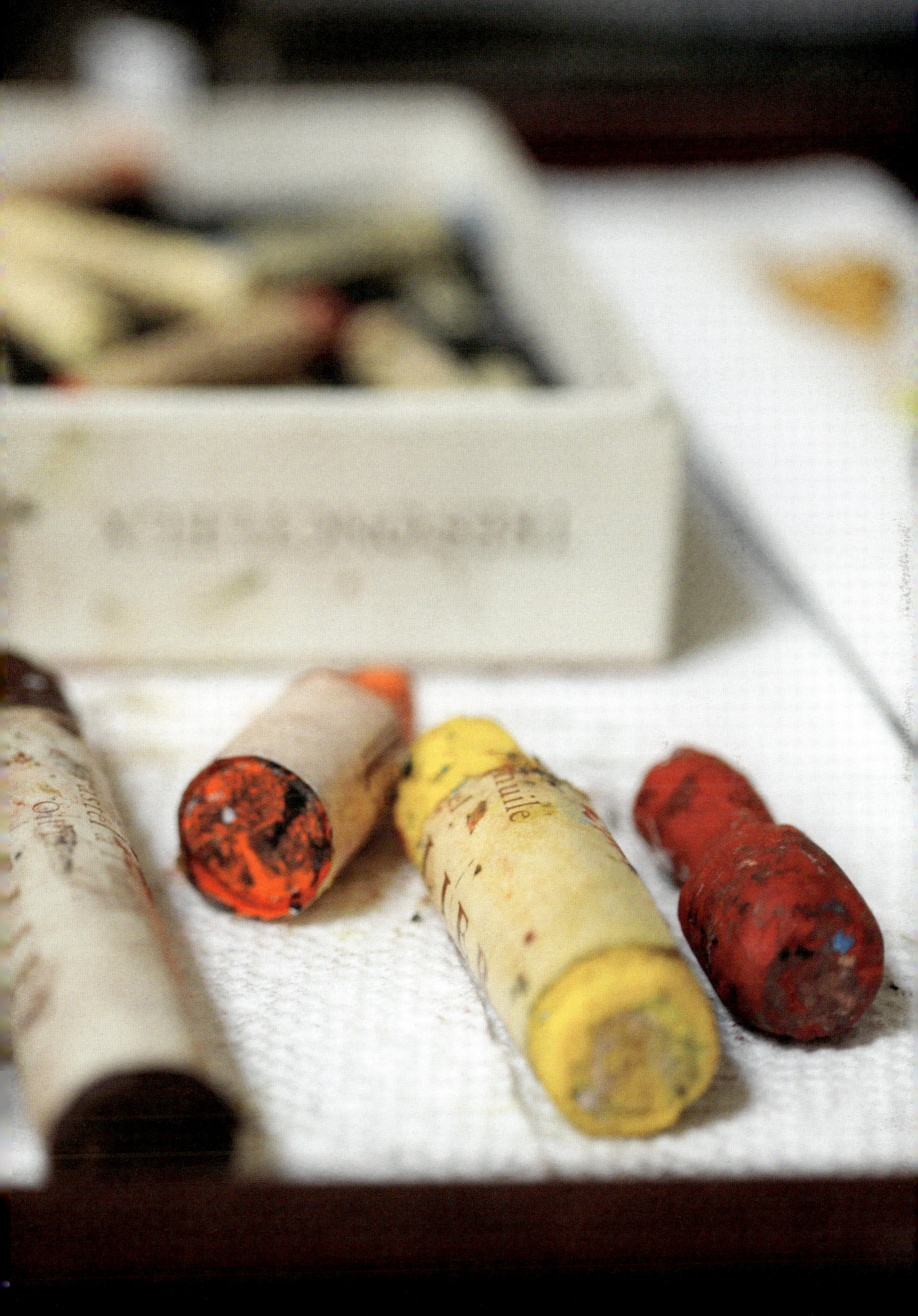
huile

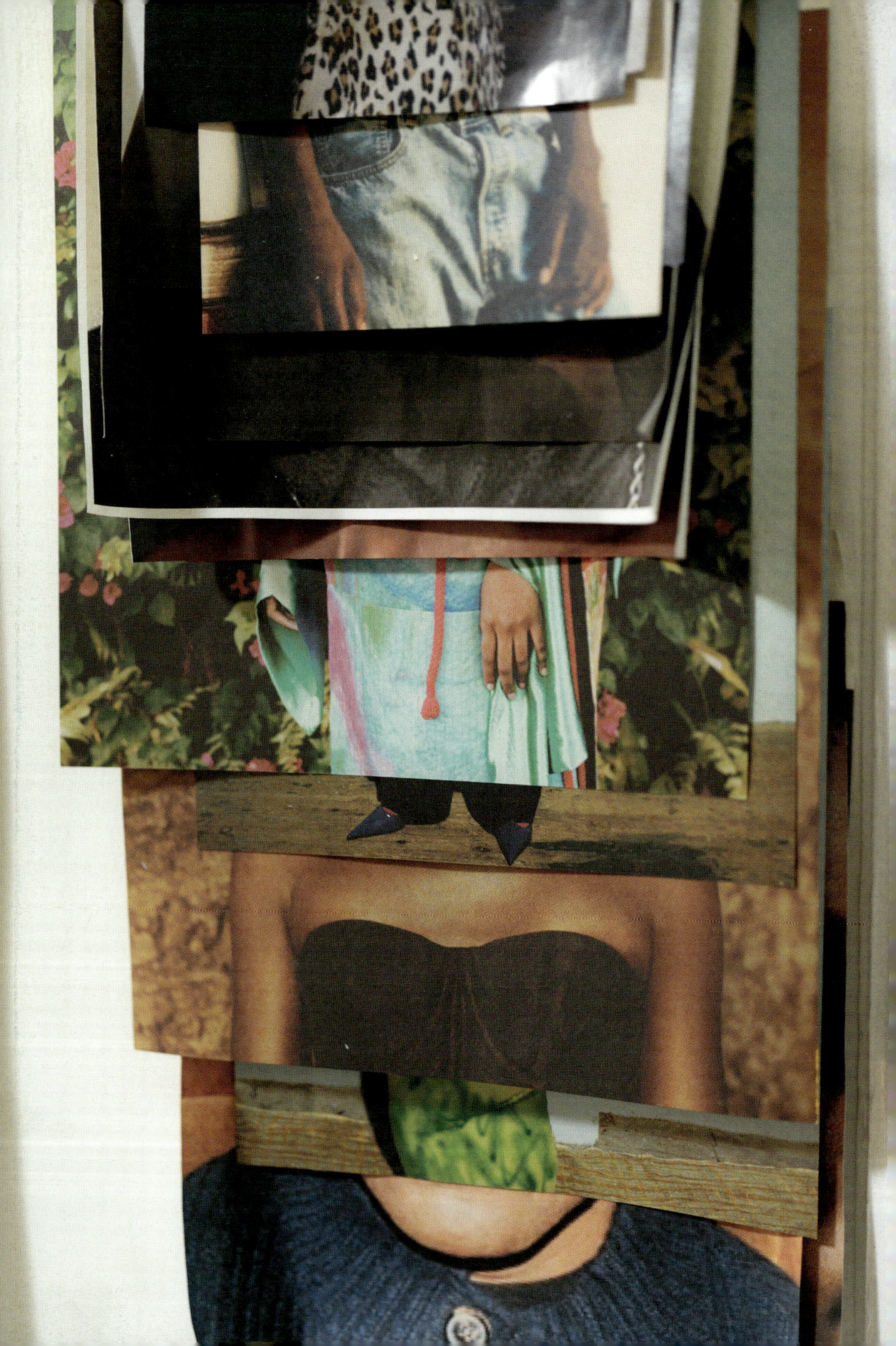

On the previous pages
p. 57
Photo by Kyle Dorosz,
Courtesy Gagosian

pp. 58–64
Photo by Maris Hutchinson,
Courtesy Gagosian

A Conversation with Nathaniel Mary Quinn

Stefania Rispoli

STEFANIA RISPOLI: It's safe to say that your talent manifested itself very early on when you taught yourself to draw as a child. You then left the suburbs of Chicago and your family to attend Culver Academies in Indiana on a full scholarship. I imagine that growing up away from your family was complex and difficult at times. Did you always know you wanted to be an artist? If you think back to those early years, were there any artists you looked up to, who intrigued you or who were masters for you?

NATHANIEL MARY QUINN: I grew up in Chicago, on the South Side, and I always knew I wanted to be an artist. I liked making images and shapes but, as a child, I didn't have a grasp of the concept of being an artist. All I knew was that I liked making shapes and figures and cartoons with crayon on paper. As I got a little older, the first artist I looked up to was my father.

SR: What kind of artist was he? A painter?

NMQ: My father was very intrigued by cowboy movies and would draw many of them. My brother Richard also knew how to draw and was into martial arts because of Bruce Lee films like *The Return of the Dragon*. I remember my brother would draw figures that looked like Bruce Lee with colorful garments, big sleeves, and the black belts. So I would say my father and my brother were the two artists I looked up to.

SR: And did they teach you?

NMQ: Before I could walk, I was drawing on the walls of our apartment. My mother spanked me to stop me from marking up the walls. One day, my other brother, Charles, stopped my mother and said: "Mom, look, the drawing is pretty good. I think he has talent!" After that, my mother would let me draw on the walls of the apartment, and then she would just wash the walls down so I could draw again and again. That was her way of supporting what was an obvious passion. Then my dad stepped in, and he would draw with me every weekend. He taught me many lessons about drawing. For instance, when you draw, you should use your entire arm as your instrument. I was always drawing from my wrist, and he said: "No, that's too limiting. You have to use your entire arm to draw. Your arm is just your arm, and your body is your instrument." Then he ripped the erasers off my pencils, and he told me: "You will never erase. Every mark you make, you make it with intention. If you make a mistake, then you find a way to do something with that mistake. But you would never erase. Because every mark you put down, you did it for a reason. And you are going to learn from making so many mistakes." He wanted me to see my problems, so that I could avoid them in the future.

SR: Maybe being conscious of your body and feeling that intention has been a life lesson.

NMQ: Yes, it was also a lesson for life. The saying goes: "You measure twice, and you cut once." You must be very well prepared. My father was illiterate, and my family was very poor. We lived in public tenement housing in Chicago called the Robert Taylor Homes. Each building was 16 floors with ten apartments, and each apartment housed a family. Everybody was poor, and on top of that, the community was very violent due to gang activity. This meant a lot of shootouts and fights and terror, on top of the poverty that was pervasive throughout the entire community. I grew up with many friends who were gang members, and I had a close affiliation with the gang, although I was never a member. I had this talent for making drawings, and my father also taught me about drawing quickly. He didn't think it should take a long time to render an image. He taught me about being present, clear, and focused. Those are the lessons I took with me in my life. It's important to have an idea of what you want to achieve.

SR: And later on? Were there artists in the Chicago scene, or New York where you've lived for so long now, who influenced you or to whom you felt close?

NMQ: My first time ever coming to New York City was to attend New York University (NYU) where I graduated in 2000, and that's when I began to come into contact with "the art world" which was brand-new to me. I remember once I was in a class, and the professor took us to the Chelsea neighborhood to visit some galleries. We went to Marlborough, where an exhibition of Gary Simmons was up. Seeing those beautiful, large works was a turning point for me. Now that I think about it, I can find a relationship between his work and the German painter André Butzer, that you just showed at the Museo Novecento. Butzer made these so-called "erasure drawings," drawings on chalkboard and then erased a little bit. While visiting the gallery, I looked on the receptionist desk and saw the prices. Up until that point, I thought art was just a hobby. I didn't know you could make it a living. It was amazing! That changed my whole mindset.

SR: How old were you at the time?

NMQ: I was 23 and had just started researching other artists. I came across the works of Jim Dine, one of my favorites. He makes those gorgeous, elegant drawings of the tools in his studio, such as hammers and ropes, and self-portraits. And then Chuck Close, Jenny Saville and John Currin. Later, I studied art history: the Renaissance, but also Impressionism and Cubism.

SR: You came into contact with European art and the historical Avant-gardes. What changed? Did moving from an instinctive talent to studying and feeding your imagination with works from the past change the way you paint?

NMQ: Art history was very different for me than the notion of the art market, with artworks being treated like objects for sale. They didn't teach that in college.

I remember discovering the paintings of the Spanish artist Antonio López Garcia in library books at The Cooper Union. Another important memory that is very dear to me happened while I was studying art at NYU. I entered a competition at the National Arts League, and I won first prize in painting. My style at that time was very different. The painting showed four men on one side of the canvas and a little boy in a silver box on the other. It was about my four brothers and me, and was based on being abandoned by my family. Four brothers were separated from me, and the box represented the institutions that gave me refuge, like NYU. When that painting won first prize, it came with a monetary award of $1,000 and I was thrilled. I then met a man who told me about his mother, a very famous artist, and he wanted me to meet her. I said I would love to, so, the weekend came and I went to the West Village, to a brownstone. He said: "This is my mother, Louise Bourgeois." She was sitting on the floor, a frail old woman, and we made drawings together. She looked at my work and said it was very, very good, and that I was very talented. The next day I went to the Museum of Modern Art and saw all her books. That's when it dawned on me, the caliber of artist she was and how blessed I had been to meet her in her home.

SR: It seems to me that nothing happened by accident. I'd like to shift our focus to your painting practice today, which has established you as an accomplished member of the art world. Your portraits recall the decomposition typical of the historical Avant-gardes, especially the Cubist collages. That revolution was the desire to make a clean sweep with what were perceived as *preconceptions* of nineteenth-century art. An idea of art based on technical know-how (knowing how to paint, how to draw, how to sculpt) and on classical aesthetic canons (harmony and balance of forms) had to be deconstructed. Artists no longer had blind faith in the objectivity of vision. The act of looking was more complex and more *decomposed* than imagined. There was no single objective way of seeing reality. Thus, art also had to reflect the complexity of both this vision and the world. It did not have to soften or sweeten reality, but rather to tell its many facets, its rawness and harshness. The collage technique responded perfectly to these needs. It was possible to introduce non-artistic elements taken directly from the real world onto the canvas, to break down and reassemble, and to suggest the presence of more levels within the same thing thanks to this superimposition of several elements. Do you find elements in common with this idea in your work and the way of *composing* figures?

NMQ: Of course, I find that my work has common points to Cubism. Collage has a very old tradition, and Cubism has pretty much impacted every artist in some way. It's like taking sculpture and making it flat. You can see everything at once. Cubism was born from a world that was changing, not just the art itself. There was a tumultuous rupture of issues that didn't only infiltrate the political space, but also the artistic space. And this went on for years. Those world-changing experiences are the equivalent, in some respects, to the tumultuous life-changing experiences that took place in my life. So, that is the foundation from which my collage style comes. When I landed upon my style, I admittedly was not very familiar with Picasso's work or Cubism. When people started writing about my work and comparing it to Cubism, I looked more to Picasso's works and realized the relationship between the two. I was not directly impacted by Cubism itself, nor was I directly impacted by Francis Bacon. I wasn't very familiar with Bacon's work, but I was familiar with the life-changing circumstances of my upbringing. Picasso was no doubt influenced in part by a combination of world changing events and his investigation of African mask making. Those two elements combined helped to create the fertile grounds for Cubism to come about. Well, it was Picasso and Braque, actually. They are very similar in style and in aesthetics, but Picasso went through an evolution. At the beginning, it was the so-called analytical Cubism, and then synthetic Cubism. The birth of these epic paintings, that really are just small paintings, was also typified in his sculptures. I tried to make an analytical cubist work because I wanted to understand how to do it. It's extremely complex and time-consuming. I said to myself, "this is why Picasso stopped making these works!" I know this may sound simplistic, but when you look at a Cubist work by Picasso, the figure is actually born out of a collection of cubes. It's the cube shape. It's easy to look at it and just marvel at the work, but when you look at it, you also see the literal cubes, and he uses the plane to implement certain shadows or lines that form a figure, like in *Man with a Guitar*. The style itself is the polar opposite of the kind of paintings that were being made prior to Picasso. Before, there were great efforts placed on artists to be loyal to the natural world as it appeared, and of course, there was great involvement with the Church.

SR: This is why Picasso and Cézanne represented a kind of revolution…

NMQ: That's it! The revolution was caused by all of this attention on following the rules and painting the natural world. Doing things the way God sees fit and following this order meant nothing because, at the end of the day, it led us into World War I. So what's the point? Let's break away from this and find something else because this way isn't working. I think it was that sentiment that gave rise to other forms of art making. People were engaged in other forms of living, in other ways of thinking about themselves, about government, about life, about everything because that old way only led to war, and millions of deaths. So, I continue on that path. For me, my collage style didn't come from looking at Picasso's or Bacon's work. It came from a need to explore the tumultuous wrath that I felt in my life as related to my family. Although my work is not collaged, I try to use this way of thinking in my work to talk about the complex world of eternal humanity.

SR: This is perhaps also the reason why you have mostly devoted yourself to portraits. Your technique is the result of very meticulous work that you have perfected over the years and that allows a perfect balance between very different souls. Is there room for improvisation? Where is it to be found? Is it a jam session?

NMQ: Well, a lot of it is already improvised anyway, so there is obviously room for more improvisation. You said it is like a jam session, and that's a good way of thinking about it because it's similar to jazz music. I have to be able to solve problems in the moment.

SR: In a way, is it related to what you said about your father and about your mistakes? Just finding a solution?

NMQ: Yes, absolutely, always find a solution and learn to embrace your mistakes. I think that's at the crux of improvisation. You are taking a risk. Are you confident enough to allow your being and your talent to take over and to trust in the path? Don't think your way through it, but rather feel your way through the process. That's what jazz musicians do when they're improvising. They're feeling their way through the sound, the rhythm and the energy around them. In my practice, improvisation equals solutions.

SR: Save your life by finding and founding a new path.

NMQ: That's it.

SR: In Florence, you exhibited both works on canvas and on paper. The latter seem to have a different lightness, also in the color palette. Do you prefer one of the two media? Do you approach them differently?

NMQ: I prefer them both. I determine if I should make a work on canvas versus a work on paper depending on how I feel about it. Based on the vision that comes to me, I feel that it should be a work on paper, or a work on canvas. I do approach them differently just based on the technical aspects of the materials. You don't want to put oil paint on paper because it can filter through the paper. However, there are things that I cannot do on linen canvas and that I have to do on paper.

SR: The materials guide you in your choices.

NMQ: To use soft pastel on canvas is tricky because the surface of the canvas may not have enough tooth to grab the soft pastel the way paper does. For the most part, my vision guides whether the work is on paper or canvas.

SR: The titles of your works seem to have a precise function and meaning for you, is that correct? They seem to give keys to your characters, as if they were elements of a story that you leave in the hands of the public.

NMQ: That's right, titles work in concert with and are meaningful to the works themselves.

SR: But do they arrive at the end of the work when the work is finished or prior?

NMQ: It's like a clue into the meaning of the work or the character being displayed. There is a new painting in *Split Face* called *The Record Player* (2023). It is two figures sitting on both sides of a record player because when I was growing up, my father had a record player and my parents would listen to it all day. It was a prized possession in our household. For us, it was a luxurious item, and my father was very proud of that record player. They used to sit and listen to stand up comedians and old Motown music, like Al Green, James Brown, or Patti LaBelle, and they sat together, just like in that image.

SR: Do accessories or uniforms have the same function? In the European portrait tradition, artists wanted to convey a very precise, idealized image of the portrayed subject. For example, noble patrons wanted to impersonate a very precise message to the public, often linked to their power and ostentation. So, the choice of costumes, accessories, poses and sets was made to respond to that precise message.

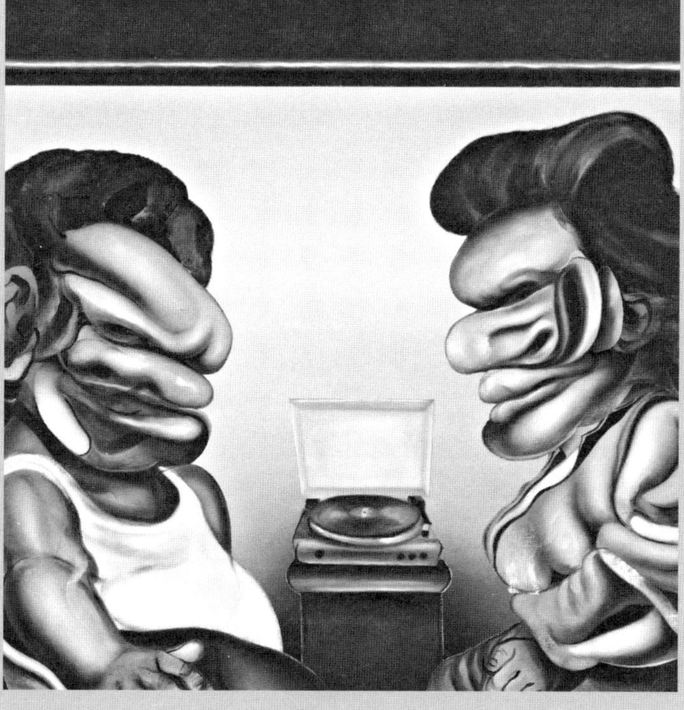

The Record Player
2023
oil paint on linen canvas stretched over wood panel
91.4 × 91.4 cm
Courtesy the Artist and Gagosian

NMQ: I use accessories and clothing as a functional, compositional thing. The clothes themselves have no meaning, but the color of the clothes has to bring a certain kind of balance to the work.

SR: They are important for the final composition.

NMQ: In the old tradition, the costumes or the garments spoke to the socioeconomic status of the sitter, and even the position they held had a meaning. In my work, that's not the case. I'm looking for clothing or images of clothing with the right kind of color and shape. So, it is really about the photograph I'm looking at. If the photo of that shirt fits the composition the right way, then it can give it balance.

SR: Behind each of your portraits there seems to be a story that combines very personal memories with events that perhaps do not relate to your own experience. *Mr. Shaw* (2023) is the guiding image of the exhibition. Can you tell us more about it? Who was Mr. Shaw and why did you decide to dedicate a portrait to him?

NMQ: After I learned that my mom had died, I returned to Chicago for her funeral. I later stayed with my grandmother for Thanksgiving and learned that my family was gone. I had been abandoned, and I was only 15 years old. Then my best friend's mother—her name is Ms. Boykins, my best friend's name was Roosevelt Boykins—made contact with my grandmother. I stayed with her, and she was taking care of an old man named Mr. Shaw. I didn't know who he was, but, for some reason, my grandmother was very loyal to this man, like she was taking care of him. Mr. Shaw couldn't move and she was like a 24-hour around-the-clock nurse for him. I don't know if Mr. Shaw was her husband, a friend, or a lover, and I never asked because I didn't know what to ask. Sometimes she would wake me up in the middle of the night so I could help her lift Mr. Shaw over, helping him out of the bed into the chair so he could watch TV. He just used to sit there all day. But then I saw these photographs, and there was a time when Mr. Shaw was a clean cut guy. He was dressed in a red hat and had a feather coming out of his jacket lapel, like one of those guys you would see in the black films in the 1960s. You could tell he was a smooth operator into making money. He might have been a ladies' man and now here he is, a statue in a bed. The only things moving were his eyes and his breathing. *Mr. Shaw* comes from that memory.

SR: We are not one thing, but rather several things at once, and each of them is the result of a relationship (with others, with the world) that is always changing. As if our body forcibly holds many parts together, sometimes one has the upper hand over others. You have a BA in art and psychology from Wabash College (Crawfordsville), and you worked for several years as an educator, so human relationships and human psychology have always played a role in your life. Does choosing to work with portraiture, and therefore with the theme of identity, have anything to do with that?

NMQ: I'm really serious about the rainbow-like spectrum of humanity because I'm really interested in human beings. Your identity is impacted by your relationships with other people and the institutions you attach yourself to. If you grew up in a church or a club, or your parents were part of some organization that they were loyal to, that will in turn change your identity. When you explore identity, what you come across often is the commonality that you share with other people. We have more in common with each other than we have differences. I think, generally speaking, you have good and wholesome people, and you have not so good and not so wholesome people. You can label it racism, sexism, whatever name you want to give it, knock yourself out. But at the end of it all, it leaves a very unhappy, mean, despairing person. That person feels worthless because a person who feels good about him or herself does not have the capacity to treat other people wrong. You hurt people because you feel hurt yourself. So, when people are in that state, they do things in the hopes of propping themselves up. Their sense of empowerment is dependent upon your sense of inferiority. It could be communicated through another form of expression called antisemitism or racism, jealousy or envy. It could come through any form of expression. But if people are able to see that we have more in common with each other than what is different, we wouldn't be that way. We would be set free. So, I find the exploration of humanity to be very real. It's honest. It truly looks

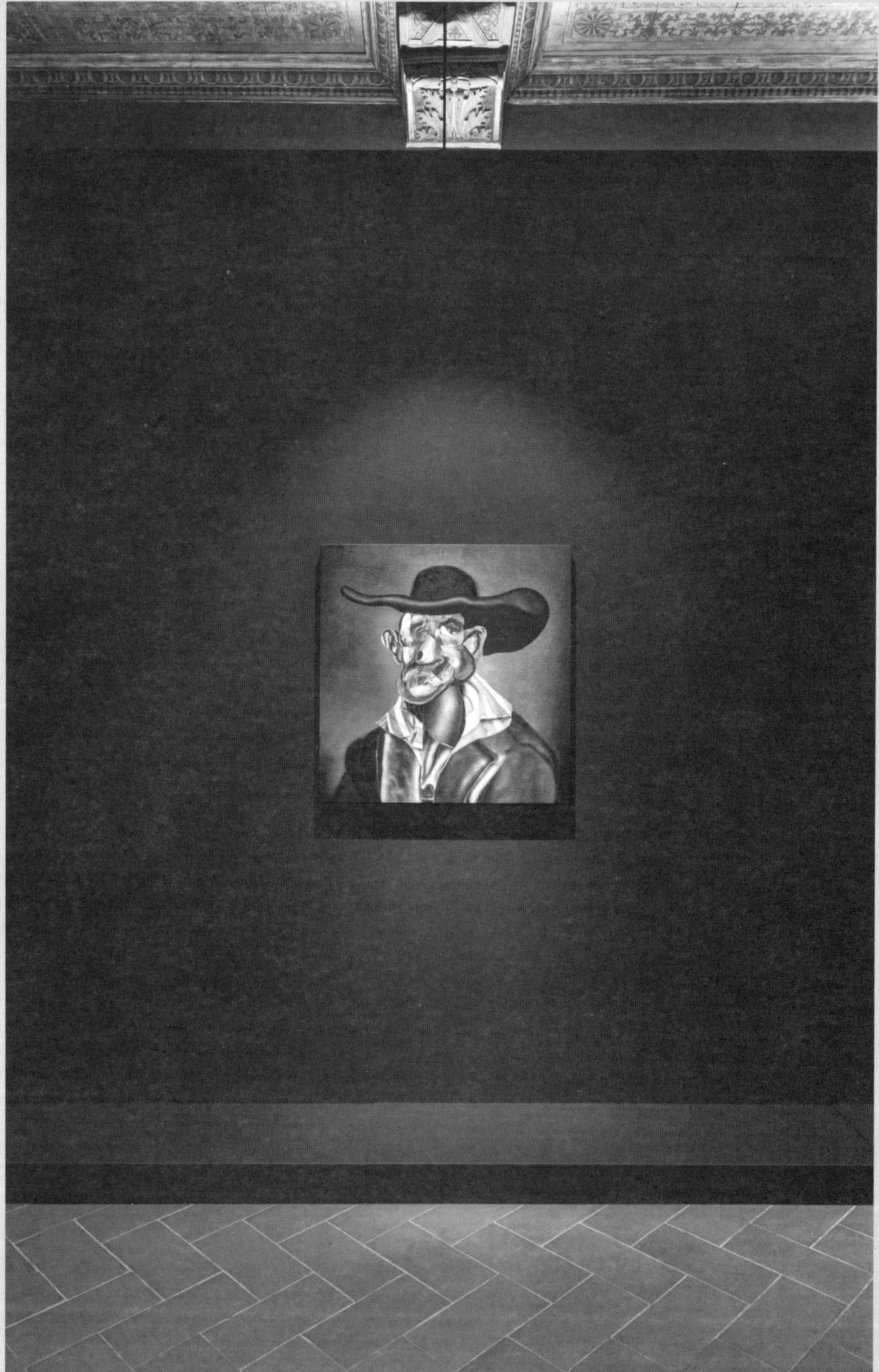

Stefania Rispoli

Mr. Shaw
2023
oil paint, oil pastel, soft pastel, gouache, black charcoal on linen canvas stretched over wood panel
91.4 × 91.4 cm
Courtesy the Artist and Gagosian

at the wounds and the Band-Aids of humanity. People remember your being, your integrity, your character, the kind of human being you are, and the way you treat other people. Including the way you treated the least of us. They don't remember how much money you made, or how many awards you won. People remember how you treat them. You know what you care about? How they treated you. How it made you feel on the inside. That's what matters. I want to paint that.

SR: What was your first experience when you entered the Museo Bardini in Florence like? Did you seek a direct dialogue with the works of the past or did you prefer that dialogue to arise from their arrangement within the exhibition? How do you relate to the works of the past?

NMQ: I wanted to make works that were in direct dialogue with some of the paintings from the collection of the Bardini Museum and to take advantage of this opportunity to try to stretch my visual language, and take more risks. I knew that Sergio Risaliti would create a dialogue between my works and those of the Museum. And so he did. I wanted every work in the show to borrow from the color palettes of the paintings from the Renaissance and the Baroque period. I wanted to borrow from the visual operations that you would normally see in paintings from that time period.

The Marcher
2023
oil paint, oil pastel, gouache on linen canvas stretched over wood panel
101.6 × 76-2 cm
Courtesy the Artist and Gagosian

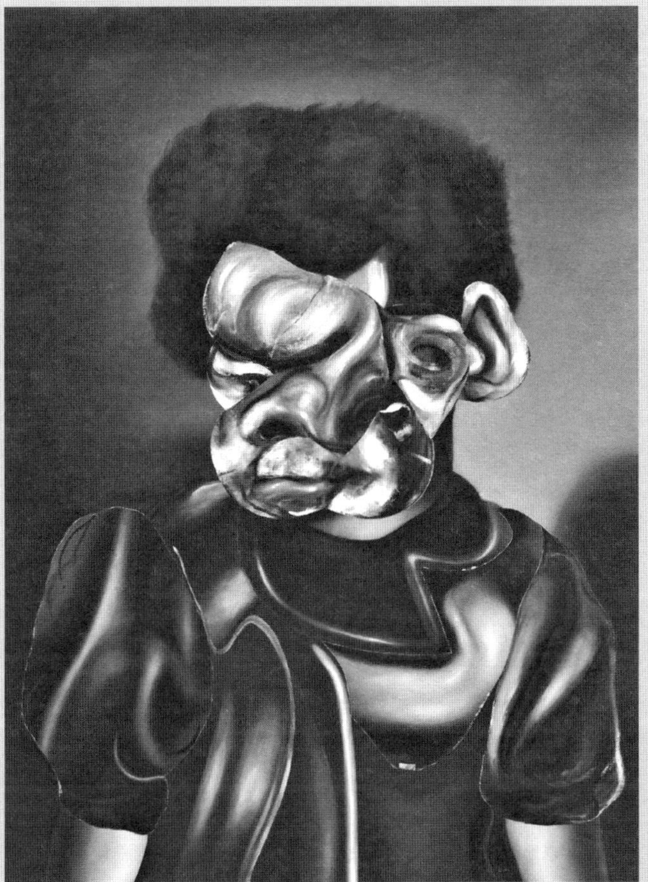

SR: Can you tell me about the new works you created for the exhibition?

NMQ: For the most part, these five new paintings are based on people I know and personal experiences. For instance, *The Marcher* (2023) is a reflection of black women who would march in different movements, like the civil rights movement. These were also women who were avid church goers. I thought it would be interesting to place a painting like that in a space like the Bardini because the museum's paintings were born from the context of a church where members were encouraged to believe in a higher power. It was a concerted thoughtful avenue that I took in wanting to make a painting like that. I wanted to place an image or representation of a black American woman in that space. The palette of the flesh was meaningful because when you look at the paintings at the Uffizi Gallery, you get the sense that the figures in those paintings are not just paintings of white, Italian people.

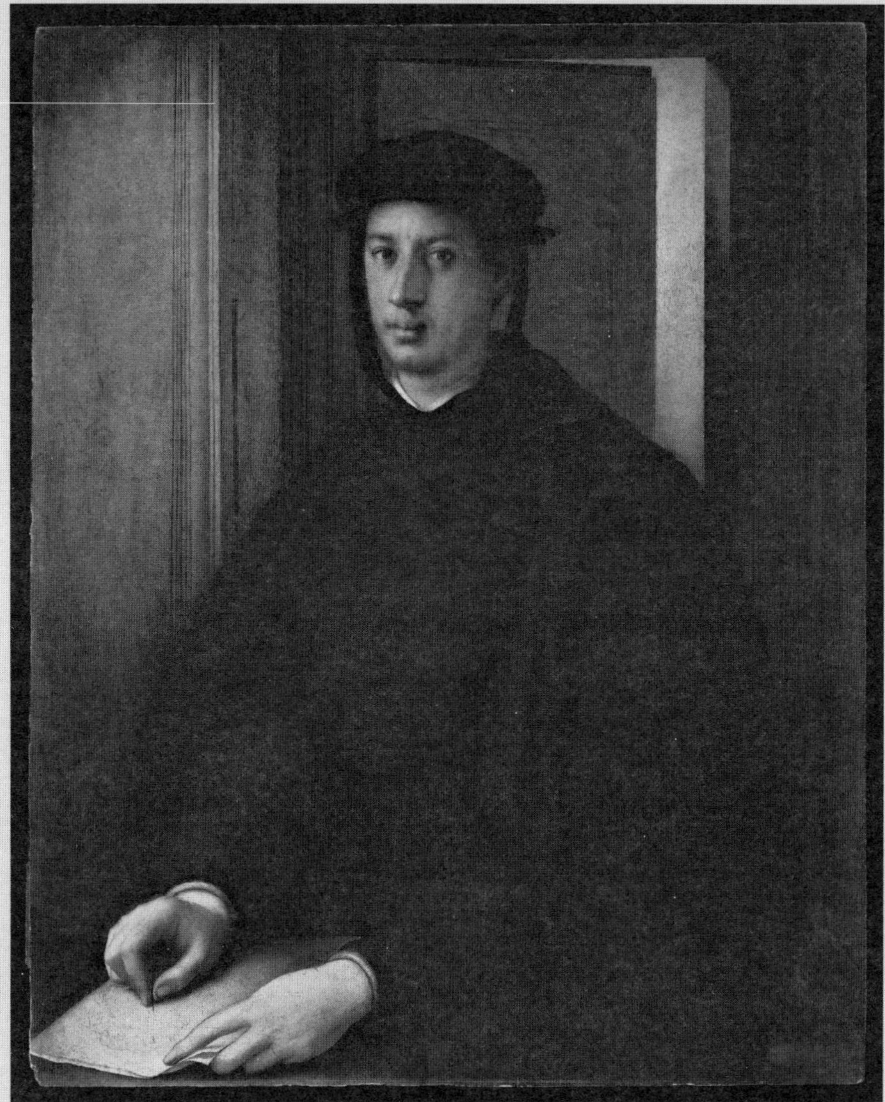

(Jacopo Carucci),
Ritratto di Alessandro de' Medici detto Il Moro, 1535,
oil on panel,
101.3 × 81.9 × 2.8 cm
Courtesy Philadelphia Museum of Art, Philadelphia

These paintings are a reflection of those in positions of great authority, and they were created as objects of worship for the lower class rather than actually trying to show love and protection. So, this is not really about race. This is about hierarchy, power, and privilege. You may think you see yourself in these paintings, but don't ever get confused. You are a lower class subject to the figures in these paintings, and that is really at the root of the color palette being used. That's the difference, that's more political. In *The Marcher*, I wanted to add my color palette to the conversation. Historically, these women were giving themselves up to a higher power as well. They went to church and they marched in the name of God, of justice and equal rights.

SR: The Renaissance portraits themselves represented the exaltation of a power and that woman in *The Marcher* is being led by a power. You also made a new work inspired by a portrait of Alessandro il Moro by Pontormo. Why did you choose that work? What was it like to paint from a portrait made by another artist in such a distant era, therefore starting from an image elaborated, digested and idealized by another author?

NMQ: Everything started from that image. I decided to focus on the face, because it's a portrait and it's a beautiful painting. I wanted to do my own remakes on it: I read more about the historical backdrop of painting and the figure, and I decided to make a painting that was really just a direct reflection of that. An homage to Florence and its history. That work belongs to a part of history where a person like me would never be able to have a show in this part of the world, so it's a testament to how far we have come as a human race. It is really a big honor to be in a show like this, and for my works to be hanging in concert with what is thought to be art historical power. This is a fact. No one today can look at the Renaissance period without reflecting on the power of art throughout history.

SR: I can say that it was a joy for us to have you in this kind of frame, because you show us a different way to look at the Renaissance, and to see what we have around us every day. And so, it was also a gift for us. Thank you again for your time, and for this conversation.

Contents

NATHANIEL MARY QUINN
Split Face

OCTOBER 7, 2023 – MARCH 11, 2024

an exhibition promoted by
Comune di Firenze

realized in
Museo Stefano Bardini
Museo Novecento

curated by
Sergio Risaliti
Stefania Rispoli – MUS.E

scientific coordination
Francesca Neri – MUS.E
Jacopo Manara

press office and comunication
Camilla Fatticcioni – Museo Novecento
Lara Facco - Lara Facco P&C
Claudia Santrolli - Lara Facco P&C
Elisa Di Lupo - Comune di Firenze

visual identity
Forma Edizioni

education department
MUS.E

graphic prints on display
Polistampa Firenze S.r.l.

photographs
Ela Bialkowska, OKNO studio (cover, pp. 1, 4-5, 8-11, 14, 16-17, 20-21, 26-27, 30-31, 36-37, 40, 74)
Owen Conway, Courtesy Gagosian (pp. 13, 25, 28-29, 35, 72, 75)
Courtesy the artist (pp. 12, 23)
Serge Domingie (pp. 43-44, 52-55)
Kyle Dorosz, Courtesy the artist and Gagosian (p. 57)
Rebecca Fanuele, Courtesy the artist and Gagosian (p. 33)
Maris Hutchinson, Courtesy Gagosian (pp. 58-64)
Rob McKeever, Courtesy Gagosian (pp. 3, 7, 15, 18-19, 38-39)
Nicola Neri (pp. 48-49)

translations
NTL – Il Nuovo Traduttore Letterario S.C.

insurance
MAG Spa - Fine Art Operational Service

handling and artworks preparation
Apice Firenze

walls preparation
Archea Associati
Cogeas S.r.l.
Passamaneria Moderna

condition report
Rossella Lari

lighting installation
Vannetti Andrea S.r.l.

room renovation
Matteo Calviani

surveillance
REAR Società Cooperativa

thanks to
Dario Nardella, Mayor of Florence
Alessia Bettini, Vice Mayor and Councillor for culture
Matteo Spanò, President of MUS.E

special thanks to
the artist, Nathaniel Mary Quinn, to all the collectors who collaborated in the realization of the exhibition, and to Donna Augustin-Quinn, Laura Andreini, Emanuele Cremona, Emily Cooper, Manuela Cuccuru, Pepi Marchetti Franchi, Antonello Martella, Elena Pinchiurri, Ashley Stewart Rödder

also thanks to
all the offices of the City of Florence involved, in particular Office of the Mayor, the Cultural Directorate, and Alessia Ballini, Andrea Batistini, Andrea Bianchi, Mariella Carlotti, Laura Chimenti, Paolo Cianchi, Silvia Colucci, Rita Corsini, Emanuele Crocetti, Gabriella Farsi, Eva Francioli, Francesco Fricelli, Marina Gardini, Ilaria Nerli, Antonella Nicola, Cecilia Pappaianni, Silvia Penna, Serena Pini, Paolo Sani, Chiara Useli, Milly Valdevies, Valentina Zucchi

the exhibition was realized with the support of
Gagosian

The catalogue has been published with financial support from the Ministry of Tourism's "Fondo siti UNESCO e città creative"

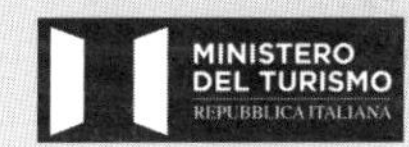

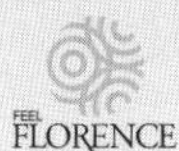

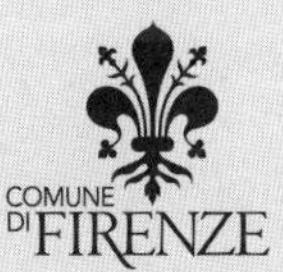

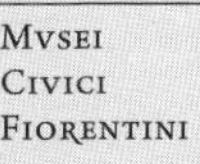

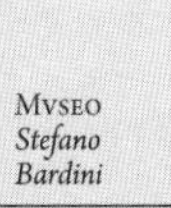

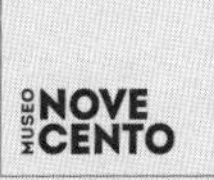

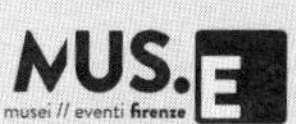

Cover
Mr. Shaw, 2023

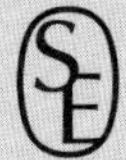

Silvana Editoriale

Chief Executive
Michele Pizzi

Editorial Director
Sergio Di Stefano

Art Director
Giacomo Merli

Editorial Coordinator
Silvia Perfetti

Copy Editing
Filomena Moscatelli

Layout
Donatella Ascorti

Production Coordinator
Antonio Micelli

Editorial Assistant
Giulia Mercanti

Photo Editor
Silvia Sala

Press Office
Alessandra Olivari, press@silvanaeditoriale.it

ISBN 9788836657353

Silvana Editoriale S.p.A.
via dei Lavoratori, 78
20092 Cinisello Balsamo, Milano
tel. 02 453 951 01
www.silvanaeditoriale.it
Reproductions, printing and binding
in Italy
Printed by Tipo Stampa S.r.l., Moncalieri (Turin)
in October 2025